Chris Keenan'
Flavours of SWANSEA

by
Chris Keenan
& Liz Barry

To Lynda and the cats

To Mum

Contents

Foreword	5
Swansea-The Culinary Capital of Wales	7
Swansea the Fishing Port	9
A Ballad of Salad	13
To Start	15
Baked Stuffed Mussels	16
Lightly Spiced Gower Parsnip Soup	18
Fresh Crab, Salmon & Laverbread Potato Cakes on a Lemon and Garlic Sauce Topped with Crispy Fried Leeks	20
Salad of Grilled Goats Cheese, with a Warm Red Onion and Raspberry Dressing	22
Oriental Duck Parcels, with a Hoi-sin and Plum Sauce	24
Smoked Chicken with an Orange and Walnut Salad	26
Mushroom and Asparagus Pancakes Topped with Pencarreg and Smoked Salmon	28
Oysters at Oystermouth	30
Cockles at Penclawdd	32
Cockle, Leek and Potato Gratin	34
To Follow	39
Braised Venison in Dark Ale and Onions, with Garlic Roasted Shallots	40
Poached Salmon with Creamed Leeks and Courgettes	42
Chicken in a Coconut and Thai Curry Sauce	44
Escalope of Pork, with a Raspberry and Mustard Seed Sauce	46
Slow Cooked, Breast of Welsh Lamb with Puy Lentils	48
Cajun Spiced Seabass with Roasted Sweet Peppers	50
Honey Baked Breast of Duckling with Glazed Apples and Cider Sauce	52
Saute of Beef in a Mustard and Pepper Sauce with Paprika Croutons	54
Welsh Lamb with Cracked Pepper and Fresh Blueberries	56
Roast Pheasant with Apple and Herb Dumplings on a Piquant Orange and Red Currant Sauce	58
Pencarreg and Vegetable Filo's with a Baked Tomato Dressing	60
Caramelised Red Onion Tart	62
The Gower Peninsula	64
To Finish	67
Hot Caramelised Pear Tart with Butterscotch Sauce	68
Mousse of White Chocolate on a Dark Chocolate Sauce	70
Russe Biscuit Filled with Fresh Fruit	72
Bread and Butter Pudding	74
Seasonal Fruit Crumble	76
Chris's Choice of Welsh Cheeses	78
To Help You on Your Way	79
Acknowledgments	83

Swansea Marina

FOREWORD *by Sir Harry Secombe.*

As a boy growing up in Swansea, there was no greater treat on a Saturday afternoon than to go shopping with my mother in the Swansea Market.

It was a wonderful place – a veritable Aladdin's Cave, redolent with the smell of fresh bread, Cockles, Laverbread, faggots and peas. The odour of new leather from the rows of football boots hanging by their laces mingling with the sugary perfumes of the mounds of toffees, marzipan, bonbons and hard boiled sweets in all sorts of shapes, from goldfish to pineapples on the Confectionery stalls. It was enough to make a young lad swoon with ecstacy.

Looking through this book has brought it all back to me and my salivary glands burst forth anew! It is the very essence of what is best in Swansea's Culinary delights and I recommend it most heartily.

And now, if you don't mind, I'm going to get Myra to have a go at the "Cockle, Leek and Potato Gratin". It sounds delicious!

Fountains in the Square

SWANSEA *The Culinary Capital of Wales*

Throughout Wales there are first class Chefs, excellent restaurants and a wealth of fresh produce, but nowhere in the Principality can boast such a concentration of all these things as Swansea.

Whether your taste is for a Wine Bar, Bistro, Formal or Ethnic restaurant, Public or Country House, you will discover outstanding examples in each category.

Naturally, this enviable situation didn't arise over night. For fifteen years or more I have witnessed the Swansea food scene evolve to its current standard. Things really started moving forward when the Chefs and Cooks of our area realised that to truly develop their skills they simply had to move away. Some went to London, others to Europe, giving them greater experience, knowledge and confidence, then to return home and cook better than ever before.

All of this was some time ago, and now those Chefs make up some of the "leading lights" of the Swansea Restaurant scene, who have themselves trained many young cooks, and attracted new talent into the area. Which can only further enhance the pleasure of dinning out in and around Swansea, for both residents and visitors alike.

Cockles and Laverbread have been a staple dish long seen on many menus, they are a cherished part of our culinary heritage, and will continue to be so, yet with the experience and expertise of the people within the industry, we are now moving forward, and gaining recognition for a far wider cuisine.

Swansea is an exciting place to cook these days, the competition from other Restaurants is very high, the customers are knowledgeable and demanding, all this of course keeps me on my toes and my motivation at a healthy level.

Local produce is featured on many menus, which is hardly surprising when you consider what we have right on our door step, the Gower Peninsula, which has a chapter of its own further in the book. Also, just a short drive from Swansea, is an area that I refer to as "my Normandy" it's actually West Wales, and is full of small villages which lend their names to food products, like Pencarreg and Llanboidy (cheeses). As well as others that are synonymous with, smokeries, fresh salmon, sewin and trout, creameries, oysters and other seafood, it is a very "foodie" area with new products coming on line all the time. It really is just like driving through Normandy, where you see road signs to places and associate them with something good to eat.

I love to keep an open mind and experiment with new dishes and ideas, making as much use as I can of local produce, then treating them with influences from all over the world and learning as I go, helps me develop further as a Chef, as I feel if you have an open mind, you will never stop learning.

I became hooked on Food, Cookery and the Kitchen from an early age, I found college too much like school, so I simply went off to London and worked my way up from the bottom. I spent about twelve years in the West End in total, as I came to the end of my time there, I was to discover, unfortunately, that the higher you go in the kitchen hierarchy, the less cooking you seem to do as it all becomes very business orientated and non creative. These days, I am busy and happy developing a Bistro in the Mumbles,"Barrows", holding a Food and Cookery Theatre at Sketty Hall on Monday evenings, which is proving to be very popular, and broadcasting on BBC Radio Wales every week, so as far as job satisfaction is concerned my cup is pretty much overflowing, and my enthusiasm for promoting good food in Wales and in particular, Swansea continues to grow.

Chris in action at Swansea Market

Many local chefs, are now known by name, by face and by their cooking styles, so they are no longer that anonymous person behind the scenes, but a personality in his or her own right.

In creating this book, I wanted to produce something more than simply a collection of recipes, it had to be a little different, special, with a blend of History, Art and Poetry and of course some superb images of the City. Choosing which recipes to include proved to be a lot more difficult than I thought, they had to be exclusive to the book, the ingredients had to be fresh, affordable and easily available from local suppliers, which includes our very own Swansea Market. They were tried and tested, they .then had to be accompanied by some excellent food photography, so to encourage people to want to make them, quite a challenge to say the least.

There are a number of flavours to be discovered here in Swansea, but for now this is my Flavour of Swansea, I hope you enjoy it.

SWANSEA *The Fishing Port*

Swansea can trace its origins back to Viking and Norman times, the name is believed to have come from the Norse words Swein's (or Svein's) Ey, meaning Swein's Island, which is attributed to a submerged sandbank in the mouth of the River Tawe. Swansea's history has always been connected with water, and was recognised as one of the Country's leading fishing ports.

Francis Greene from Coakley Greene, Fishmongers, of Swansea Market was able to recall this exciting and important part of Swansea's history.

"I remember with a little nostalgia the old Swansea Fish Market on the South Dock, which is now the Swansea Marina, and the fleet of trawlers named after famous Welsh Castles, Conway, Caerphilly and Oystermouth to name but a few. They were sturdy vessels fuelled by coal; there was something strangely romantic about them.

They were owned and run by a parent company Consolidated Fisheries of Grimsby and the skippers and fishermen who sailed in them were a special breed, mainly from the Swansea area. Brave men, they had to be to face the horrendous seas they encountered. They were generous and warm hearted, but tough men, mostly heavy drinkers.

They only had thirty six hours ashore with their families, then back to sea for fourteen days. They sailed away from the South Dock with wives and sweethearts waving goodbye, with many a tear being shed. They would fish mainly in the sea area of Shannon, off the South Coast of Ireland, sadly sometimes they never returned.

The sea coast of Shannon was a big fishery for hake, the fishermen brought back tons of it, as well as megrin, plaice and cod, but hake was the number one fish caught. That is why the Swansea housewife became orientated to hake and gave it to her family; this influence still prevails today. On the fish market in the 1930's it sold for 3 pence per pound, compared with £2 per pound today, even more for jumbo cutlets.

I became fascinated with the fish market on the South Dock, the hustle and bustle, water and ice everywhere, the smell of fresh fish being landed. The fish itself had bright eyes, firm flesh, looked good, exciting, with a smell hard to describe as it smacked of the sea.

My biggest fascination was with the trawlers themselves, I got to know every one of them, their rusty hulks were somehow beautiful to me. At every opportunity I would jump on my bike and ride

Little red boat

to the Dock just to look at them. My interest did not go unnoticed by the fish merchants who knew I was the grandson of Mrs Coakley, and it was not long before a fourteen day trip was arranged on a trawler during my school holidays.

It was to be a trip of a lifetime. I sailed on the Caswell Castle and I never forgot it; Darkie Jimmy was the Skipper, Mr Green was the Cook, who by coincidence also had a son called Francis.

By the time we steamed off Lundy Island on our way to the Irish Sea, I was violently sea-sick. We were in a Force Ten gale that raged for two days, I thought I was dying. The hardened seamen felt sorry for me and continually gave me cups of tea that were as thick as soup, but when I got over it I ate like a horse, and even got caught pinching a piece of cake from the galley, and got told off for it.

You cannot explain the experience of seeing the net being hoisted aboard and the Mate releasing the fish from the "Cod-end". The noise from the sea, the hundreds of seagulls and gannets greedy for food is indescribable. Throughout the night the process carried on, the deck would be floodlit, and it is a miracle the fishermen did not get swept overboard; of course sometimes they did.

On the way back home the vessels would catch loads of Dublin Bay prawns, but a lot were dumped overboard because there was no market for them. You see, we had not become sophisticated in our tastes in those days; now with our travels abroad we all know the taste of scampi, which is of course, Dublin Bay prawns.

Before the 1939 war, Swansea was a prosperous fishing port, so much fish was landed of all species that it was recognised as one of the leading fishing ports in Britain. Fish were sent to Billingsgate, Manchester, Liverpool, Leeds, all the major cities in the U.K., and even exported to France. To expedite the transportation, special fish wagons would be hooked onto the back of express trains, ready to be loaded after the fish auction.

Sadly, because of over-fishing especially for hake, the fishery of the South Coast of Ireland in the Shannon area was destroyed. It became uneconomic to maintain the fleet in Swansea, so the parent company recalled the vessels to Grimsby in 1956. That signalled the demise of Swansea as a major fishing port, at that time employing between five and six hundred men.

Today only a handful of small vessels operate out of Swansea Docks, but they bring in some useful fish for the consumer, mainly plaice, skate, whiting and "dovers". It only represents ten percent of our total fish sales, the rest is supplied from other fishing ports across the Country - Aberdeen and Peterhead in Scotland, Newlyn, Plymouth, Brixham and Looe on the South Coast, also Hull, Grimsby, Lowestoft and Fleetwood.

Of course we are fortunate on the Gower Peninsula to have stocks of crab and lobster which are always in demand, and especially the famous sea-bass which is available to us particularly in the Summer months - probably the finest fish of all.

The Old Swansea Fish Market

Swansea's most famous son, Dylan Thomas

A BALLAD OF SALAD

I cannot eat the red, red rose,
I cannot eat the white;
In vain the long laburnum glows,
Vain the camelia's waxen snows,
The lily's cream of light.

The lilac's clustered chalices
Proffer their bounty sweet,

In vain; though very good for bees,
Man, with unstinted yearning, sees,
Admires, but cannot eat.

*Give me the lettuce that has cooled
Its heart in the rich earth,
Till every joyous leaf is schooled
To crisply crinckled mirth;*

*Give me the mustard and the cress,
Whose glistening stalklets stand
As silver white as nymphs by night
Upon the coral strand;*

*The winking radish round and red,
That like a ruby shines;
And the first-blessing, onion shed
Wher'er your lowness dines;*

*The wayward tomato's glorious head,
Cool cucumber sliced small;
And let the imperial beetroot spread
Her crimson over all.*

Though shrinking poets still prefer
The common floral fashions,
With buds and blossoms hymn their Her,
These vegetable loves would stir
A flint-heart's mineral passions.

                              Dylan Thomas

"A Ballad of Salad" was first published in the Swansea Grammar School magazine, in July 1929, when Dylan Thomas was 14 years old.

This is believed to be the first time republished since 1929

to Start

Crammed with food the table creaks.
The Dogs grow fat on the crumbs.
God bless our board that springs no leaks,
And here no ruffian comes,

Vernon Watkins
(from 'Ballad of the Mari Lwyd' 1941)

Baked Stuffed Mussels

Fresh Mussels cooked with a little wine, garlic and herbs are quite simply superb. Quite often I would finish the resultant juices with cream, for a more luxurious dish. But sometimes it's good to do something a little different with them, like this.

THIS IS WHAT YOU NEED
SERVES 4

3 LB LIVE MUSSELS, CLEANED
AND READY TO USE.
3 OZ CHOPPED SHALLOTS.
SPRINKLE OF FRESH CHOPPED PARSLEY.
1PT SALSA.*
PEPPER CORN CRUMBLE MIXTURE.*
DASH OF DRY WHITE WINE.

THIS IS WHAT YOU DO

Pour the live mussels into a large pot, add the shallots and dry white wine with a sprinkle of chopped parsley, cover with a lid and place over a high flame. As soon as the mussels open, remove from the heat and strain.

Break off the empty side of the shell and place onto the serving plates, discarding any that have not opened.

Once all four plates have sufficient mussels, heat up the salsa, check the seasoning, and fill each mussel shell. Next top each mussel with a sprinkle of the crumb mixture and bake in a oven or place under a hot grill until golden brown, serve with a good wedge of lemon.

*See "To Help You on Your Way" section

Lightly Spiced Gower Parsnip Soup

I love to prepare parsnips in all sorts of ways whether it be pureed, roasted, baked, mashed in with potatoes, minced and added to game casseroles during the cold months, or as here in a soup. When buying parsnips, don't be put off by those that have been affected a little by frost as these are often the very sweetest ones.

THIS IS WHAT YOU NEED
SERVES 4 - 6

6 OZ POTATOES, WASHED, PEELED AND DICED.
1LB PARSNIPS, WASHED, PEELED AND SLICED.
4 OZ CHOPPED ONIONS.
2 CLOVES OF CRUSHED GARLIC.
3 OZ BUTTON MUSHROOMS.
1 TEASPOON GROUND CORIANDER.
1 TEASPOON GROUND CUMIN.
5 FL OZ DRY WHITE WINE.
2½ PINTS OF LIGHT CHICKEN STOCK
10 FL OZ WHIPPING CREAM.
LITTLE OIL FOR COOKING.
SALT AND PEPPER.

THIS IS WHAT YOU DO

Firstly, heat a little oil and add the chopped onions and garlic, cook these gently until the onions begin to soften a little. Add the parsnips, potatoes and the mushrooms together with the spices, turn the heat up and cook these together for a good few minutes whilst stirring in order to get the most out of the spices.

Pour in the dry white wine, reduce this by half before adding the stock or water, season a little, bring to the boil and allow to simmer gently for fifteen to twenty minutes, or until the parsnips soften. Pull to one side and allow to cool.

Once cooled, put the entire contents of the pot through a blender until good and smooth, pour back into the pot, set to simmer then add the cream. Check the seasoning and serve topped with a few crisp croutons.

If you would like your "lightly spiced parsnip soup" a little spicier, just add a teaspoon full of green Thai curry paste towards the end, it has a wonderful effect.

Fresh Crab, Salmon & Laverbread Potato Cakes on a Lemon and Garlic Sauce Topped with Crispy Fried Leeks

Whether they are for a relaxed little lunch with friends, or as a starter to a formal dinner "fish cakes" can rise to the occasion. With this sauce and garnished with the crispy fried leeks they certainly take on a little sophistication.

THIS IS WHAT YOU NEED
SERVES 4 - 6

1LB MASHED POTATOES, STILL WARM.
1 SMALL CLOVE OF CRUSHED GARLIC.
8 OZ POACHED SALMON.
(KEEP THE STOCK).
8 OZ FRESH CRAB MEAT,
HALF WHITE, HALF DARK.
2 HEAPED TEASPOON LAVERBREAD.
1 PINCH OF GROUND CORIANDER.
1 PINCH OF GROUND CUMIN.
1½ OUNCES BUTTER.
4 OZ CHOPPED ONIONS.
DASH OF DRY WHITE WINE.
2 EGG YOLKS.
SPRINKLE OF MIXED HERBS.
SEASONING.
A LITTLE EXTRA BUTTER FOR FRYING.

THIS IS WHAT YOU DO

Melt the butter in a pan until sizzling, add the chopped onions and crushed garlic and cook until tender, sprinkle in the mixed herbs then moisten with just a dash of wine. Add this to the mashed potatoes, mix well.

Mix into the potato mixture, the egg yolks, spices and the laverbread, making sure that all the ingredients are well incorporated at each stage. Next mix in the crab meat and the seasoning. Now carefully add the flakéd salmon, mix in gently so you don't break up the flakes too much.

The best thing to do now, is to chill the mixture in the fridge or freezer for about half an hour as it will then become easier to handle.

That done, divide into eight equal quantities, roll into balls then place onto a floured work surface. With a palette knife shape into cakes, then fry in butter until golden on both sides. Serve with Lemon and Garlic Sauce.*

*See "To Help You on Your Way" section

Salad of Grilled Goats Cheese, with a Warm Red Onion and Raspberry Dressing

Goats cheese has a fabulous mild fresh flavour, and once grilled a creamy texture, then married to toasted pecans or pistachio nuts, juicy dark grapes and a piquant fruit dressing – well I could eat it all day.

THIS IS WHAT YOU NEED
SERVES 4

FOR THE DRESSING

2 OZ PEELED RED ONION.
2 DESSERT SPOONS OF RASPBERRY VINEGAR.
1 TEASPOON GRAINY MUSTARD.
7 FL OZ EXTRA VIRGIN OLIVE OIL.
1 DESSERT SPOON OF CLEAR HONEY.
SALT AND PEPPER.

FOR THE SALAD.

A BOWL OF CRISP SEASONAL LEAVES, ENOUGH FOR FOUR.
8 SLICES OF GOATS CHEESE, 2 OZ EACH.
20 TOASTED PECAN HALVES.
20 LARGE BLACK GRAPES (SEEDLESS IF POSSIBLE).

THIS IS WHAT YOU DO

For the dressing, simply place all the ingredients into a food processor until its all nice and smooth.

For the salad, place the washed and dried leaves onto four serving plates. Place the goats cheese on a non-stick frying pan and place under a hot grill until golden brown, arrange on top of the salad. Then to the pan, add the required amount of dressing and the grapes, then warm gently. Pour this over the cheese salads, finish with the toasted pecans and serve.

As an extra topping, caramelised red onions are an excellent option. See page 62

Oriental Duck Parcels, with Hoi-Sin and Plum Sauce

This is a very popular starter, and is one of my favourites when I am giving cookery demonstrations. Many people seem a little nervous about working with filo pastry, but once you brush it lightly with a little melted butter, its a whole lot easier to handle.

THIS IS WHAT YOU NEED
SERVES 2 (4 PARCELS)

1 COOKED DUCK BREAST, 7-8 OZ.
2 OZ CHOPPED ONIONS.
6 OZ COURGETTES.
2 OZ SLICED BUTTON MUSHROOMS.
2 OZ GREEN PEPPER, CUT INTO SMALL DICE.
2 OZ RED PEPPER, CUT INTO SMALL DICE.
2 OZ BABYCORN, CUT INTO RINGS.
4 TEASPOONS HOI-SIN.
2 TEASPOON PLUM SAUCE.
2 FL OZ DRY WHITE WINE.
2 OZ MELTED BUTTER.
8 FULL SHEETS OF FILO PASTRY, CUT IN HALF.
LITTLE OIL FOR COOKING.
HAVE A LITTLE EXTRA PLUM AND HOI-SIN ON HAND.

THIS IS WHAT YOU DO

Cut the courgette in half lengthways, then in half again, cut across to form triangles. Heat a drop of oil in a shallow frying pan, add the vegetables and cook together over a high heat until they begin to soften. Add the hoi-sin and plum sauce, keeping the pan good and hot, stir everything together so its all well mixed, moisten with the wine then pour into a fresh container to cool.

To the pan, bring 2 fl oz of water to the boil, stir in 2 teaspoons of plum sauce and 4 teaspoons of Hoi-Sin serve this with the parcels.

Cut the duck breast in half lengthways, then slice across to form small thin slices.

Lay a sheet of filo pastry onto the worktop, brush lightly with melted butter, place another sheet on top brushing with butter in the same way.

Spoon some of the vegetable mixture into the centre of the pastry, place several slices of duck breast on top. Carefully lift all the corners of the pastry and bring them together with a gentle twist, ensuring that the filling is sealed. Repeat this process until all the ingredients are used up.

Place onto a lightly buttered baking sheet, dab a little butter on top of each parcel, sprinkle with sesame seeds and bake in a medium hot oven for ten to twelve minutes. Serve with the Hoi-Sin and Plum sauce.

Smoked Chicken with an Orange and Walnut Salad

You can go out and choose from a huge selection of smoked food these day's with private smokeries popping up all over the place. Smoked lamb, sewin and garlic are high on my list of favourites, but smoked chicken is so moist, packed with flavour I had to include it.

THIS IS WHAT YOU NEED
SERVES 4

8 OZ SMOKED CHICKEN.
3 OZ CHOPPED SHALLOTS.
3 OZ CHOPPED WALNUTS.
DASH OF FRESH LEMON JUICE.
2½ DESSERT SPOONS GOOD THICK MAYONNAISE.
LITTLE SALT AND PEPPER.
A FEW EXTRA WALNUT HALVES FOR GARNISHING.
THE SEGMENTS FROM ONE ORANGE.
SELECTION OF CRISP SEASONAL SALAD LEAVES.
OLIVE OR WALNUT OIL.
SPRINKLE OF PAPRIKA.
SALT AND PEPPER.

THIS IS WHAT YOU DO

Remove any skin from the smoked chicken, and cut the meat into a fine dice.

Place the diced chicken in a mixing bowl, add the chopped shallots, walnuts and lemon juice, stir all these together before introducing the mayonnaise. Mix well check the seasoning, spoon the mixture into four ramekin dishes, cover and place in the fridge.

Now simply toss the salads in a little olive or walnut oil, with a sprinkle of salt and freshly ground pepper and arrange onto the four starter plates.

Take the chicken mixture from the fridge, turn out onto the salads, then garnish with halved walnuts and orange segments. As you can see in the photograph a sprinkle of paprika and a few pools of the salsa does a nice job of completing the dish.

*See "To Help You on Your Way" section

Mushroom & Asparagus Pancakes Topped with Pencarreg and Smoked Salmon

I usually offer this as a starter in the evenings or as a light main dish at lunchtime, served with a salad and buttered new potatoes. The inclusion of delicious Pencarreg, an organic, soft full cream cheese from West Wales always creates interest, and deservedly so.

THIS IS WHAT YOU NEED
SERVES 4

2 OZ CHOPPED ONIONS.
4 FL OZ DRY WHITE WINE.
5 FL OZ VEGETABLE OR LIGHT CHICKEN STOCK.
1 OZ GRATED CHEDDAR.
DASH OF LEMON JUICE.
4 OZ SLICED BUTTON MUSHROOMS.
4 OZ BLANCHED FRESH ASPARAGUS, TRIMMED AND CUT INTO ONE INCH LENGTHS.
10 FL OZ WHIPPING CREAM.
SALT AND PEPPER.
2 OZ SLICED SMOKED SALMON.
4 OZ PENCARREG CHEESE.
LITTLE SUNFLOWER OIL FOR COOKING.
PANCAKE BATTER.*
A LITTLE PAPRIKA.

*See "To Help You on Your Way" section

THIS IS WHAT YOU DO

Choose a shallow saute pan, heat a little of the oil and cook the onions until they begin to soften, add the mushrooms, stir and cook together for a couple of minutes before adding the asparagus. Moisten the pan with the wine, reduce it a little then pour in the vegetable stock, allow it to simmer then introduce the cream. While it is all simmering gently, sprinkle in the grated cheddar cheese, the dash of lemon juice and a little salt and freshly ground pepper.

Lay a pancake on each plate, spoon an amount of the mushroom and asparagus mixture into the centre then carefully fold the pancake, making sure the overlap is on the underside.

Pour a little of the liquid from the mixture over the top of the pancake arranging some of the mushroom and asparagus pieces around the plate.

Place a thin slice of the soft cheese over the pancake and glaze under a hot grill. Just before serving lay a folded slice of smoked salmon to one side of the cheese and a half slice of lemon dipped in paprika on the other side.

OYSTERS *at Oystermouth*

Back in 1986, when I had the honour of presenting the very first Food and Cookery Festival held at the Patti Pavilion on Oystermouth Road, all talk of food fairs and festivals were a new idea to me, locally at least, but I could not have been more mistaken. It turns out that during the 1850's Oyster Fairs were held each September, at the start of the season. They were organised by the boat owners for the Oyster Dredgers, and were provided with bread, cheese and beer, as whole families joined in the festivities which included great celebrations, sports such as donkey and sack racing, and "climbing a greasy pole". It was a very festive occasion, and later in the day, the taverns did a roaring trade.

During its heyday (1850 - 1873) oyster dredging at Swansea Bay and all along the South Coast of Gower was a thriving industry with as many as six hundred men working on one hundred and eighty skiffs based at Oystermouth alone. It is probably best described by Revd. Kilvert of Clyro near Hay-on Wye, who whilst on holiday in Oystermouth wrote in his diary dated 18th April 1872: *"A great fleet of oyster boats which had been out dredging, was coming round the lighthouse point with every shade of white and amber sails gay in the afternoon sun as they ran into their moorings under the shelter of the great harbour cliff".*

Despite many oysters being sold outside the area, they were very much part of the local diet, being prepared in many ways; some would be coated in breadcrumbs and fried until crisp, or become the stuffing in a carpet-bagger steak. Other methods of cooking them include pan-frying with bacon, or a delicious omelette of sea-fresh oysters (a personal favourite of mine).

As many as twenty thousand oysters per boat were landed at Oystermouth, with each boat making two trips a day if they so desired. The catch would be stored in "perches", which were areas of sand divided by walls built of pebbles, with a floating log to mark each territory. These would stretch right along the beach just above the low water mark, facing the village, so that as each oysterman returned from his trip he would steer his skiff towards his "perch" and tip the prized delicacies into it. There they would stay until sold.

These were prosperous times for all involved, as at the height of the season the oystermen could earn £6 per week. They received nine shillings for every one thousand oysters, with the boat owners taking their cut, and the wholesalers selling them on for twenty five shillings per thousand in London and other English cities. The boat builders as well as the dredge makers would be kept busy, and the oyster bars and taverns along the sea-front would be lively to say the least.

With the reputation for both quality and quantity of local oysters spreading Nation-wide, oystermen with bigger, more modern boats were arriving from all over the country, particularly those who worked the Thames oyster-beds. In fact, thousands of local oysters were taken back with them not to sell, but to re-stock their own beds ! More and more outsiders came, some all the way from France, and presented serious competition to the local oystermen.

By 1875 overfishing soon became apparent, and despite rigorous restrictions being put in place, the oyster-beds were left sadly depleted. The outsiders soon left when it was no longer profitable for them, leaving locals to feel the pinch, finding it difficult to earn £1 per week. Things got worse when the beds were damaged by pollution from the new industries located in the Swansea Valley, and real poverty set in, this called for soup kitchens being set up at Oystermouth.

A considerably smaller oyster trade continued for several years, with twenty skiffs working the beds, and two hundred oysters a day being a good catch. Then in 1920 a Europe-wide virus set in and ended it all completely.

As I sit back and review the previous two paragraphs, I cannot help but pause with a little sadness and think of the people involved : the characters, the good days, the bad days, the bread, cheese and beer at the Oyster Fair, the "great fleet of oyster boats" which Kilvert described so graphically. If only they were still there, the oysters I mean. Could the beds be re-stocked ? There IS talk of it. Now there IS something to think about !

Skiffs in the bay

COCKLES *at Penclawdd*

Any visitor to the Gower Peninsula or Swansea would sooner or later hear about the cockles at Penclawdd. It is the only coastal bed in Britain which is hand picked, and has been part of the history of Swansea Market since the last century.

Della Williams is one of the few remaining cockle women, now in her seventies, she retired in 1989 after fifty one years, gathering cockles since she was eleven years old. Della can trace her family back through three generations of cockle pickers.

She recalls:" We used to carry the cockles in a large wooden tub on our heads, people used to say that they were not welsh cockles unless they were carried in this way. In the beginning it was difficult, but you became skillful at balancing it on top of a rolled tea-towel, hidden beneath a felt hat. My grandmother also carried two baskets, one under each arm. The women would come to their front doors with a basin ready for the cooked cockles, measured out in half pint glasses".

Once gathered, the cockles would be boiled in large aluminium pans over an open fire on the beach, then washed thoroughly with fresh water from taps along the top of the beach. This was to make sure all the sand was washed away. They would be stored in a stone shed at the side of the house ready for market the next day.

Gathering the cockles was not always easy, Della recalls:" During the Second World War, we had to collect the cockles by night, as throughout the day the Burry Estuary was used as a firing range. That meant that as soon as darkness fell there would be about fifty ponies and carts making their way across the sands. If the moon was up, we were lucky, though your eyes soon adjusted to the darkness, as we slowly followed each other. The older people knew the track of the sands, everyone looked out for each other and you made sure that no-one was left behind."

"At sixteen I worked for six months at the tin-plate works at Penclawdd, where I met my husband Haydn, from Gowerton. In 1947, along with my mother and step-father we set up a small cockle factory. In came a machine for sorting out and sieving the cockles, no more fires on the beach. Now the cockles were steamed and we had a cold room and refrigerators for storage".

" It was hard work, bending over for five to seven hours a day, and out in all weathers. Of course women did not wear trousers like today, always skirts. Before wellingtons we had to wear men's boots, and there were no rubber gloves to keep our hands warm and dry, though we didn't think about those things-it was just part of our lives, and there was a great community spirit".

"Today many of the old families have died out, and the younger generation have moved further afield. But the cockles will always hold some interest for anyone who pays a visit to Swansea Market and samples this delicacy from Penclawdd, and of course all the local people know how good they taste, especially cooked simply with laverbread and bacon".

Sifting the sands

Cockle, Leek and Potato Gratin

I created this dish for the very first Swansea Cockle Festival, which has since developed into a major event each September with many activities taking place in and around Swansea Market.

THIS IS WHAT YOU NEED
SERVES 4 -6

8 OZ PEELED, COOKED WAXY POTATOES, CUT INTO ¼ INCH DICE.
1 TEASPOON OF GRAINY MUSTARD
2 OZ CHOPPED ONIONS.
MUSTARD AND HERB CRUMBLE*
4 OZ FINELY CHOPPED LEEKS.
8 OZ FRESH COOKED COCKLES.
4 FL OZ DRY WHITE WINE.
5 FL OZ LIGHT FISH STOCK.
5 FL OZ WHIPPING CREAM.
DASH OF LEMON JUICE.
SEASONING.
LITTLE BUTTER OR SUNFLOWER OIL FOR COOKING.

THIS IS WHAT YOU DO

Heat the oil, or butter in a heavy bottomed frying pan. Fry the potatoes until they take on a nice golden colour all over, add the chopped onions, stir these in with the potatoes then pop in the leeks, cook these together, stirring frequently until the leeks just begin to soften.

Stir in the cockles, pour in the dry white wine and allow to reduce by about half, before adding the fish stock, simmer for a couple of minutes then add the cream.

Reduce, season to taste, add a dash of fresh lemon juice and the mustard, spoon into the serving dish, top with some of the "mustard and herb crumble", glaze under a hot grill and enjoy.

*See "To Help You on Your Way" section

The Penclawdd Cockle Beds are still worked today, and the shellfish are featured on menus throughout the Principality and beyond, as Penclawdd cockles are sold all over England and even exported across Europe.

Selwyn's Penclawdd Sea foods of Llanmorlais is a fifty year old family business run by Alyson and Brian Jones. Alyson told us how her father -in- laws business has developed from one donkey, to a fleet of vans selling the local delicacy, and expanding to markets further afield.

Selwyn's father died when he was twelve, with two young siblings to support he left school and accompanied his mother along the sands of Penclawdd to harvest the cockle beds. Not an easy task, searching the surface for the tell tale ridges of the breathing holes, the key to finding the cockles. Once discovered they would be scraped to the surface, by a hand held rake, then sieved and rinsed in a pool of water before collecting.

This is more or less the same procedure which takes place today, except a tractor and trailer have replaced the donkey and cart.

Brian, his son, followed in his footsteps, leaving school at fifteen. When he married Alyson she also became involved in the business, which then consisted of an old Nissen hut where the cockles were cooked. They saw the potential for selling the cockles further afield, bought a refrigerated van, and began going to open air markets. Week after week their customers returned, and they built up quite a reputation. This led to selling the cockles at fetes, carnivals and also at the Royal Welsh Show.

They realised there was a great demand for the cockles, and developed the business by selling through wholesalers, reaching fish mongers, smaller shops and also clientele in the catering trade. Cockles reached London, Birmingham, Devon and Cornwall, as well as West Wales, and the customers became used to the sweet taste of the Penclawdd Cockle, regarded as better than any other in Britain.

When Brian and Alyson are not working in the factory, or out in the vans selling, they can be seen down on the marshes gathering the cockles. Two more figures amongst the many gatherers silhouetted against the horizon, bending over the familiar sands looking for the mature cockles, usually about two years old. These are easily distinguished by the rings on the shell, just like those on a tree.

Today the third generation are entering the business, Ashley aged sixteen, certainly plans to carry on the family business along with his sisters Hayley (twenty two years old) and Beverly (eighteen years old).

The industry is now automated, once the original picking is over the cockles are graded, the small ones are sold locally, and the larger ones exported. They all go through the processing plant, are washed, cooked then lightly salted and heat sealed in vacuum bags, then loaded into refrigerated vehicles to continue their journey to the consumer, delivered on the same day as they are picked.

Selwyns Cockles sell as far afield as Spain, which has a large market for fish products. Never the less on weekends you will still find one of their vans in many of the out door markets across the area. The local customers never have to travel far to sample the sweet tasting cockles of the Penclawdd Marshes.

Sunset over the estuary

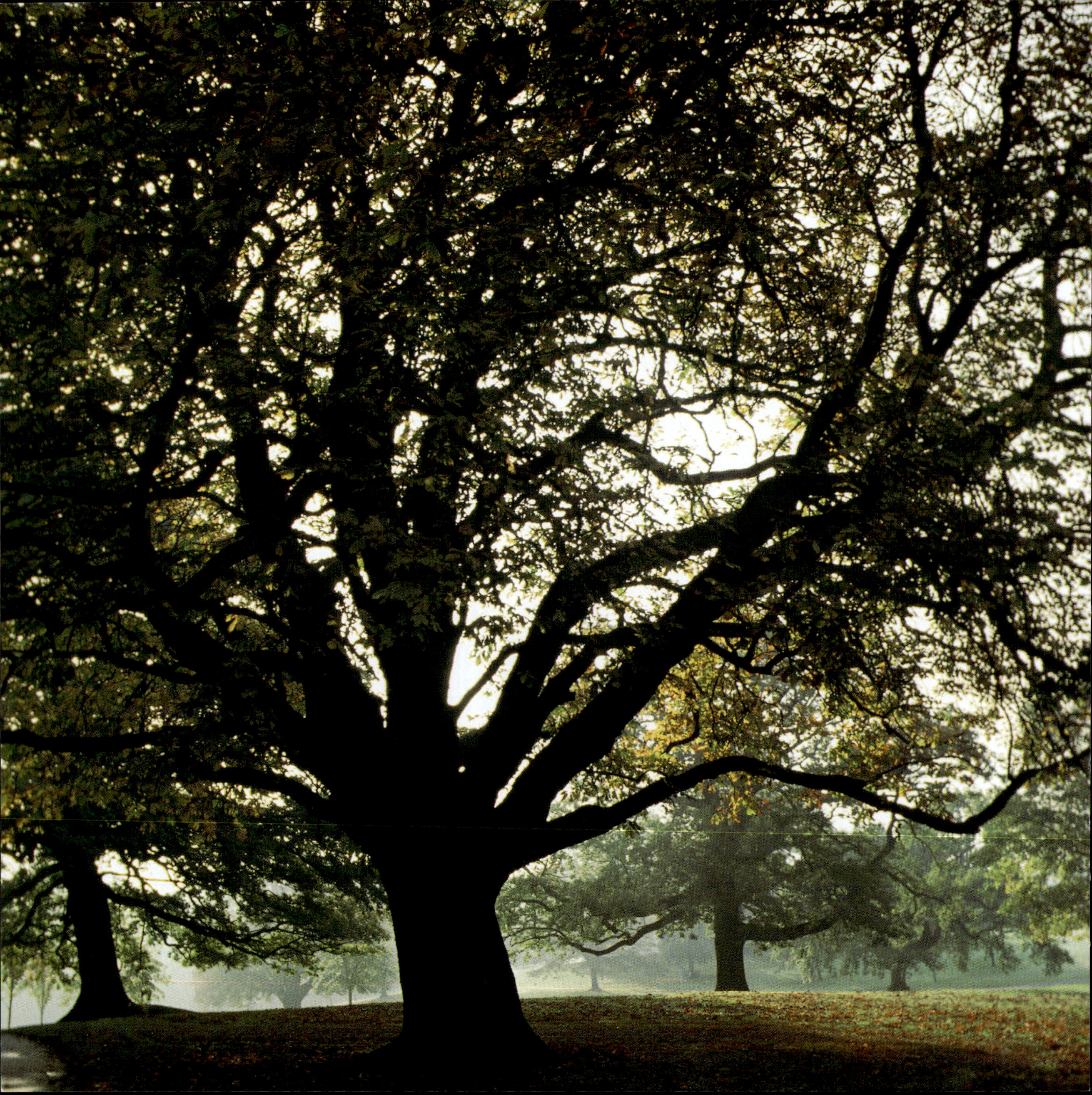

to Follow

From Beynon Butchers in Coronation Street, the smell of fried liver sidles out with onions on its breath. And listen! In the dark breakfast-room behind the shop, Mr and Mrs Beynon, waited upon by their treasure, enjoy between bites, their every morning hullabaloo, and Mrs Beynon slips the gristly bits under the tasselled tablecloth to her fat cat.

Dylan Thomas

Braised Venison in Dark Ale and Onions, with Garlic Roasted Shallots

THIS IS WHAT YOU NEED
SERVES 4.

1½ LB DICED VENISON.
2 RASHERS OF SMOKED BACK BACON CUT INTO STRIPS (LARDONS).
6 OZ CHOPPED ONIONS.
2 LARGE CLOVES OF GARLIC CRUSHED.
SPRINKLE OF MIXED HERBS.
4 FL OZ DARK ALE OR STOUT.
4 FL OZ RED WINE.
1½ PINTS WATER OR BROWN STOCK
6 OZ MINCED FRESH VEGETABLES, MADE UP OF CARROTS, PARSNIPS AND CELERY. (2 OZ EACH)
4 TEASPOONS OF TOMATO PUREE.
2 OZ BROWN SUGAR.
SEASONING.
A LITTLE OIL FOR COOKING.

TO GARNISH YOU WILL NEED
4 OZ OF SAUTEED MUSHROOMS.
16 WHOLE SHALLOTS, ROASTED SLOWLY WITH SALT AND PEPPER, A LITTLE OIL AND ½ CLOVE OF CRUSHED GARLIC.

THIS IS WHAT YOU DO

Choose a heavy pot or casserole suitable to be used in the oven. Heat a little oil in the pan, season the meat then add it to the hot pan, stirring well so that each piece becomes nicely sealed. Add the bacon, garlic and chopped onions allowing them to brown with the meat, keeping the pan good and hot so that all the ingredients are frying together. Next sprinkle in the minced vegetables, stir these in so they begin to cook with the meat.

By adding the ingredients at set stages i.e the meat, then the bacon, onions and the garlic, followed by the minced vegetables, it helps to extract the maximum flavour out of them.

Now pour in the ale and the wine, allow to reduce by half before adding the water or brown stock. Bring to the boil, set to simmer then add the brown sugar, tomato puree the seasoning and the herbs, cover with foil or a tight fitting lid and set to cook slowly in a medium oven for between one and a half and one and three quarter hours.

Once the cooking time is up, return to the stove, check seasoning then lift the meat out and place onto the serving plates. Reduce the cooking juices down to the desired consistency then pour over the venison, garnish with the roasted shallots and the mushrooms, and a few crispy croutons..

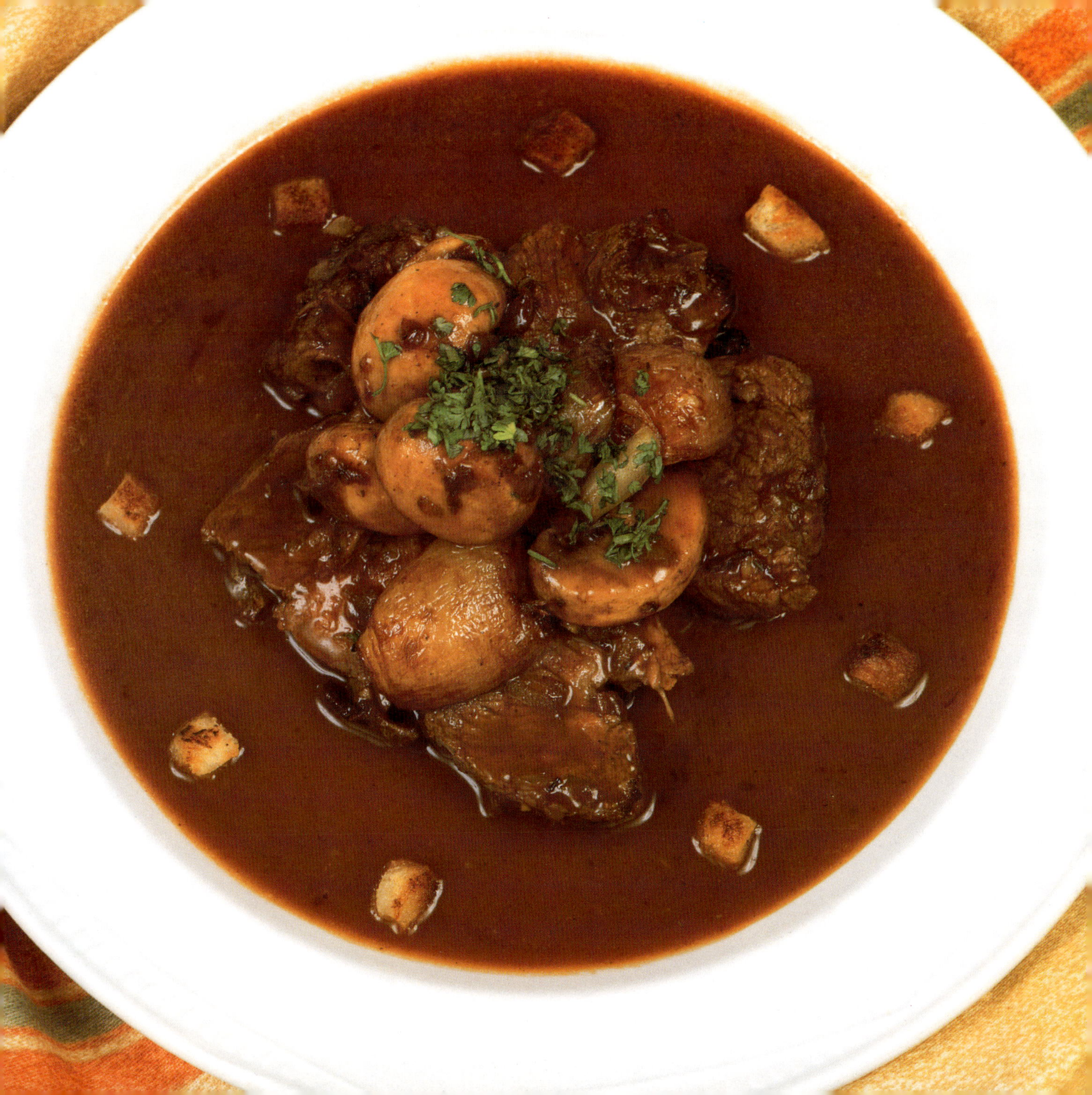

Poached Salmon with Creamed Leeks and Courgettes

The combination of leeks and salmon, is a marriage made in heaven, and the courgettes add their own crisp texture to the overall dish. This recipe works well with hake and cod, as well as sewin when in season.

THIS IS WHAT YOU NEED
SERVES 2.

2 ESCALOPES OF FRESH SALMON.
6-7 OZ EACH.
2 OZ CHOPPED SHALLOTS.
4 OZ CHOPPED LEEKS. (BLANCHED)
5 FL OZ WHIPPING CREAM.
SEASONING.
I SMALL COURGETTE. THE GREEN CUT INTO MATCHSTICKS.
DASH OF VERMOUTH.
LITTLE FRESH LEMON JUICE.
SEASONING.
PINCH OF TURMERIC OR SAFFRON.

THIS IS WHAT YOU DO

Choose a shallow pan with a diameter that the two escalopes of salmon fit into quite tightly, so they cannot move about too much during cooking. Sprinkle the fish with the chopped shallots, pour in some cold water, just so the salmon is ¾ covered. Add a little salt then cover and simmer gently over a low to medium flame, for about 5 minutes. Remove the cover, add the cream and finely chopped leeks. Reduce this down to a good consistency. Lift out the salmon escalopes, and place onto the serving plates. Finish the sauce with a little saffron or turmeric, just to give a warm glow, a dash of vermouth and a twist of lemon juice. Pour the sauce, through a strainer, over the salmon. Arrange the courgettes as shown, and place the creamed leeks on top.

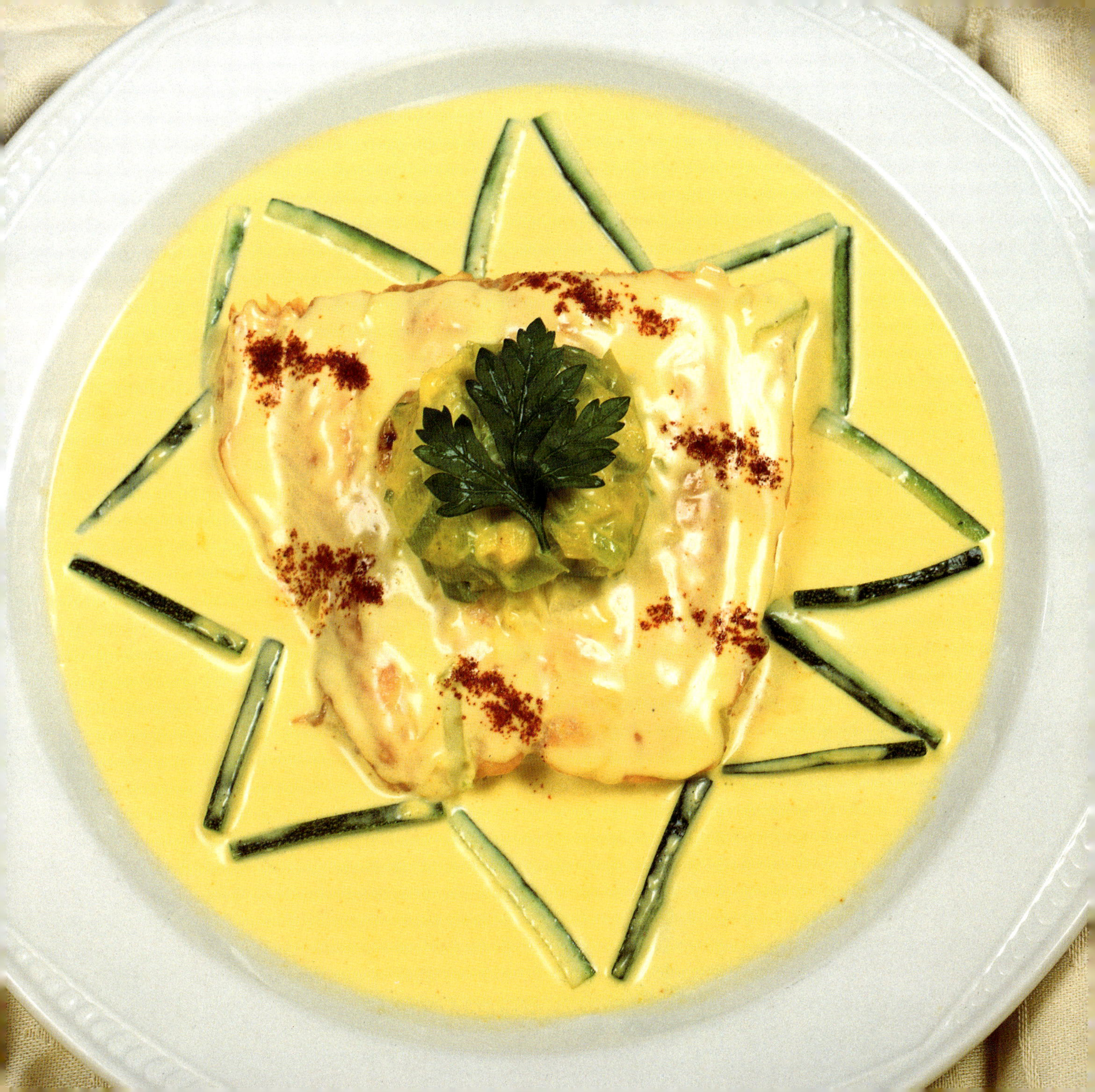

Chicken in a Coconut and Thai Curry Sauce

Some times its great to have a meal armed only with a fork, one you can really get stuck into, perhaps as a working lunch or for supper in front of the T.V.. This is one of those dishes.

THIS IS WHAT YOU NEED
SERVES 4

1½ LBS OF DICED CHICKEN.
(LEG MEAT, OFF THE BONE).
4 OZ CHOPPED ONIONS.
1 SMALL GREEN PEPPER.
CUT INTO ½" SQUARES.
2 CLOVES OF CRUSHED GARLIC.
4 TEASPOONS DESICCATED COCONUT.
3 TEASPOONS GREEN THAI CURRY PASTE.
5 FL OZ DRY WHITE WINE.
10 FL OZ BASIC JUS-LIE.
10 FL OZ WHIPPING CREAM.
2 HEAPED TEASPOONS TOMATO PUREE.
DASH OF FRESH LIME JUICE.
A LITTLE SESAME OIL FOR COOKING.

THIS IS WHAT YOU DO

Heat a little of the oil in a thick bottomed pan, drop in the peppers, followed by the onions, and garlic. As soon as the peppers begin to cook add the green Thai curry paste, give a good stir to mix well then add the diced chicken, stirring to make sure that everything is nicely incorporated.

Remember that it is important to keep the pan good and hot all the way through the above stage, so that the ingredients "stir-fry" together rather than boil.

Moisten the pan now with the wine, add the coconut and simmer for a minute or two then add the jus-lie, closely followed by the cream, tomato puree and a little seasoning. Simmer gently now and reduce down to a good consistency, finish with a dash of lime juice check the seasoning and serve with fragrant basmati rice. Garnish with a small bunch of coriander and a couple of wedges of fresh lime.

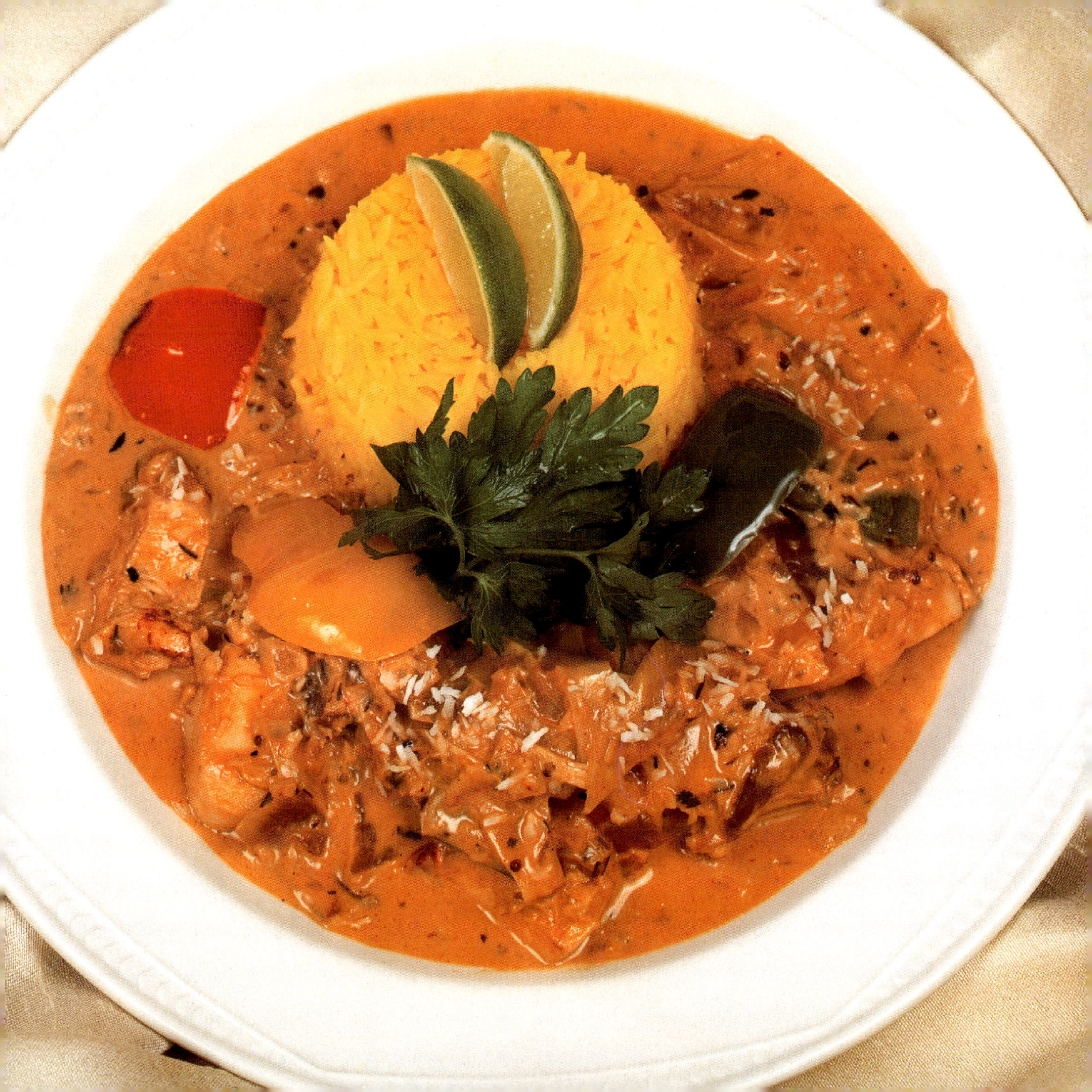

Escalope of Pork, with a Raspberry and Mustard Seed Sauce

This is a lovely dish and I often do it with Wild Boar, but in order to offer real value for money at the bistro, pork fits the bill nicely Now its not simply a case of pouring the made up sauce over the cooked pork, the pork escalopes are actually cooked within the sauce, the result is a particularly moist meat and a more flavoursome sauce.

THIS IS WHAT YOU NEED
SERVES 2.

2 SIX OUNCE PORK ESCALOPES.
2 OZ CHOPPED ONIONS.
2 FL OZ RASPBERRY WINE VINEGAR.
4 FL OZ DRY WHITE WINE.
10 FL OZ JUS-LIE.
5 FL OZ WHIPPING CREAM.
2 TEASPOONS GRAINY MUSTARD.
SALT AND PEPPER.
LITTLE OIL FOR COOKING.

THIS IS WHAT YOU DO

Heat just a dribble of cooking oil in a frying pan, place the seasoned pork escalopes in and cook for 4-5 minutes on each side allowing them to colour a little. Add the chopped onions and raspberry vinegar and let it evaporate almost entirely before pouring in the wine, reduce a little then add the jus-lie . Cover the pan and simmer for a couple of minutes. Add the mustard and the cream and simmer gently uncovered, check the seasoning and consistency then serve, garnished with some fresh raspberries. If fresh raspberries are not available, don't worry as they only serve to garnish the dish, it tastes just as good without them.

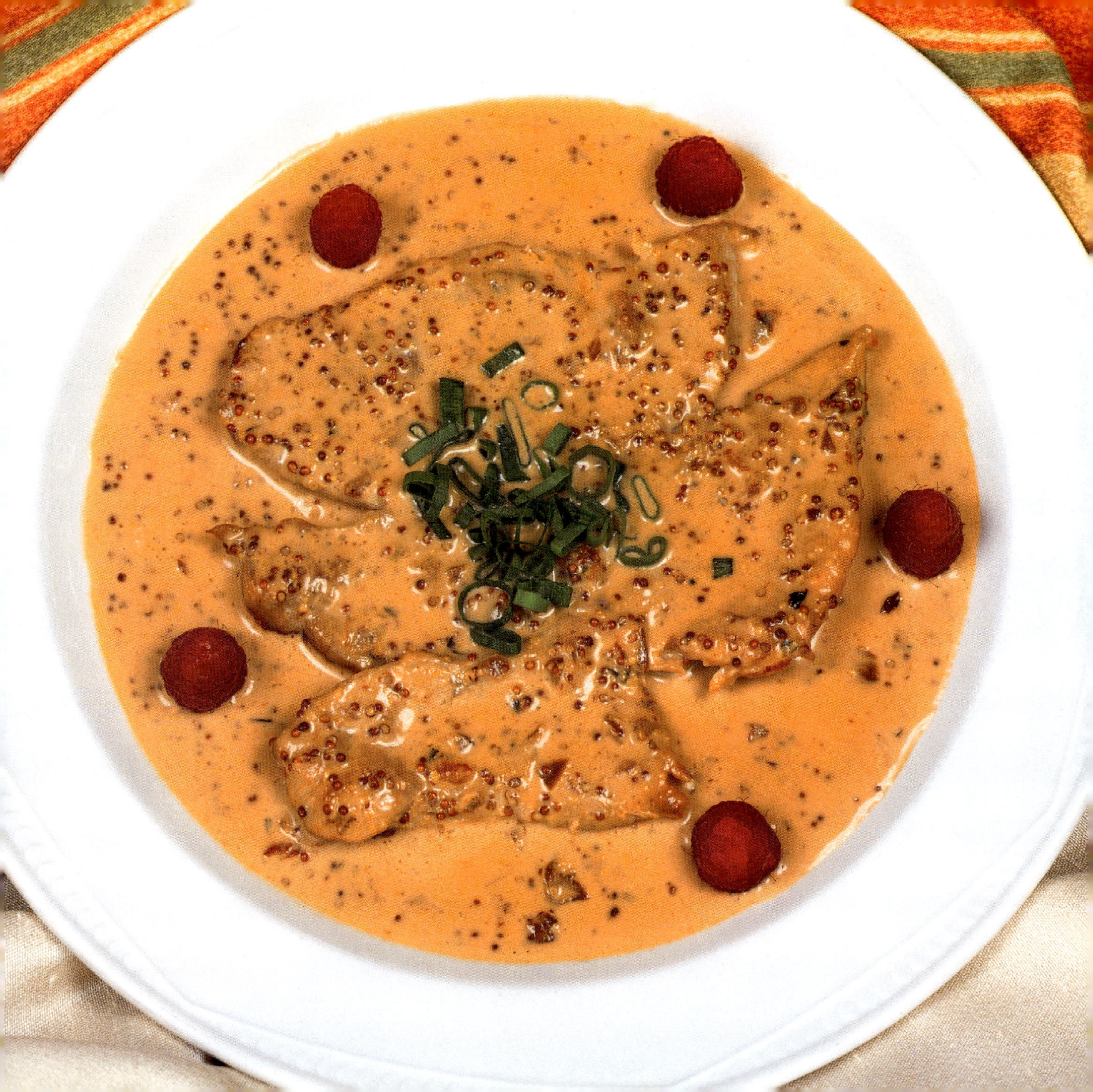

Slow Cooked, Breast of Welsh Lamb with Puy Lentils

If like mine, your butcher makes his own sausages, ask if he would stuff the breasts of lamb with a really tasty sausage meat. The lentils in this recipe are special, as they don't break up whilst cooking, therefore adding to the texture of the dish.

THIS IS WHAT YOU NEED
SERVES 4.

4 STUFFED BREASTS OF WELSH LAMB.
6 OZ MINCED RAW VEGETABLES.
(CARROTS, LEEKS AND PARSNIPS).
4 OZ CHOPPED ONIONS.
1 LARGE CRUSHED CLOVE OF GARLIC.
5 FL OZ DRY WHITE WINE.
2 OZ LENTILS (PUY).
2 PINTS OF WATER.
4 HEAPED TEASPOONS OF TOMATO PUREE.
LITTLE OIL FOR COOKING.
SALT AND PEPPER.
LITTLE FLOUR.

THIS IS WHAT YOU DO

In a good sized casserole heat a little oil until good and hot, add the minced vegetables, the garlic and onions, giving them a good stir over a high flame. Leave them to cook together for 5-6 minutes or until they begin to colour.

In the meantime, in a separate pan heat a dribble of oil, flour the seasoned breasts of welsh lamb and seal them all over so they are nicely browned.

Add the lamb to the casserole, mixing in gently with the vegetables, then pour in the wine, reduce a little before adding the water. Bring to the simmer, add the tomato puree and the lentils, check the seasoning, then cover and cook in a medium hot oven for 1 hour 45 minutes.

At the end of the cooking time, remove the lamb from the pot and place one on each plate remembering to remove any string that they may have been tied with, check the seasoning and consistency of the sauce, then pour over the lamb.

Garnish with some glazed vegetables, and serve with creamed potatoes.

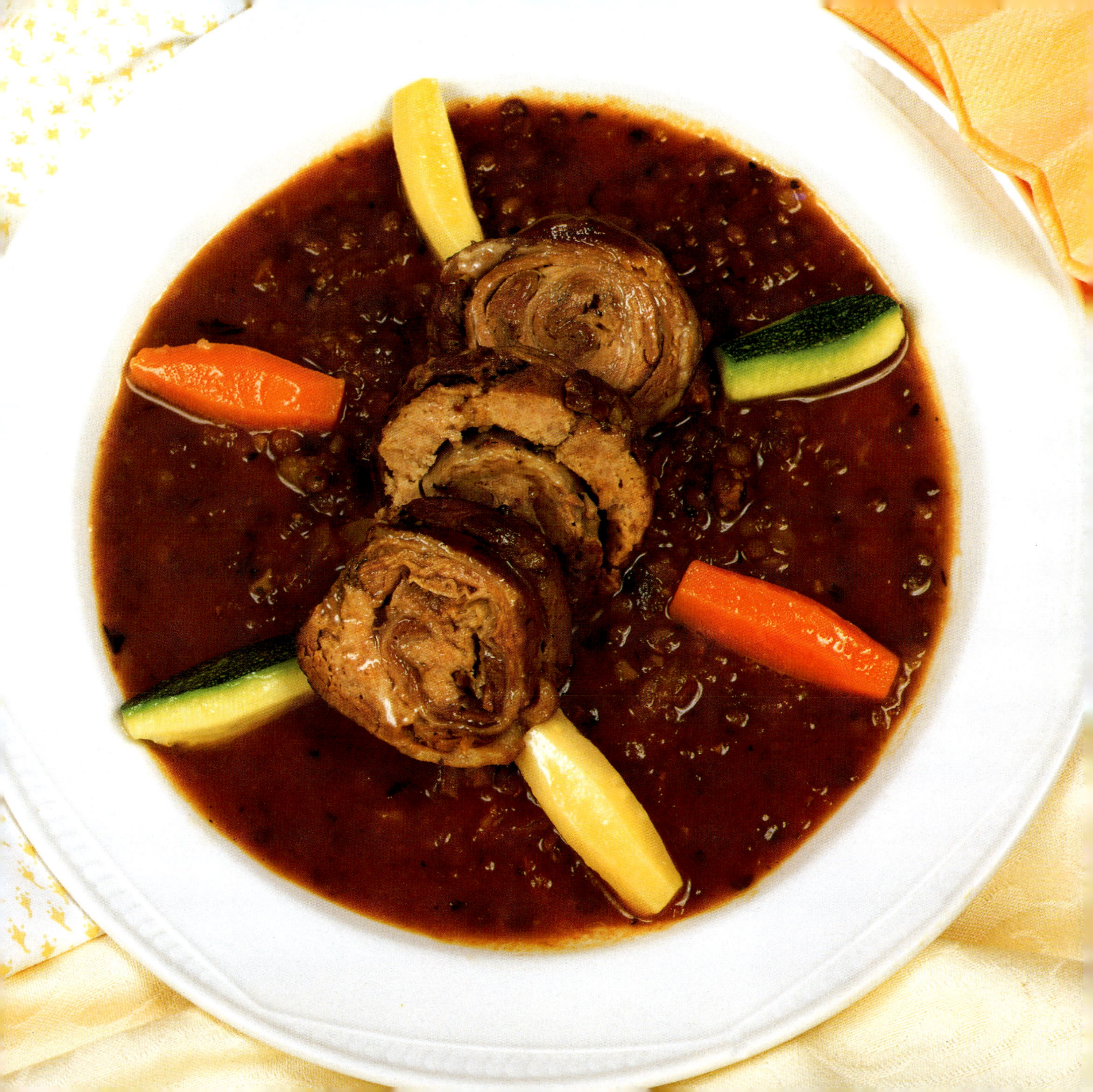

Cajun Spiced Seabass with Roasted Sweet Peppers

Cajun spices have a superb flavour, and the seabass handles them really well. This recipe is probably based on the classic Louisiana dish "blackened fish" but is not nearly so spicy. The Cajun Spices are a ready made spice mix and are easily available from most local food stores.

THIS IS WHAT YOU NEED
SERVES 2.

2 WHOLE SEABASS 1LB EACH, ALL CLEANED, SCALED AND TRIMMED.
CAJUN SPICES.
SMALL PEPPERS, ONE OF EACH, RED, GREEN AND YELLOW. CUT INTO ½ INCH SQUARES.
LITTLE SALT.
FLOUR FOR DUSTING.
½ PINT OF SWEET PEPPER SALSA.*

THIS IS WHAT YOU DO

Score the fish, by making two or three shallow incisions across the sides of the seabass, now dust them with flour, rub with a little oil, then rub in some cajun spices all over the fish, just half a teaspoon on each side will be plenty.

Place onto a baking sheet, sprinkle the peppers on top with a little salt and place in a hot oven. Once they start sizzling, give them eight to ten minutes on each side, stirring the peppers into the juices as you go.

Set each fish and the peppers onto a serving dish. Spoon the cooking juices into a small pan, add the salsa and simmer, check the seasoning and serve with the fish.

This recipe can be used with "fillets" of fresh salmon and hake as well as seabass, though you would probably be better off to grill rather that roast these smaller cuts.

*See "To Help You on Your Way" section

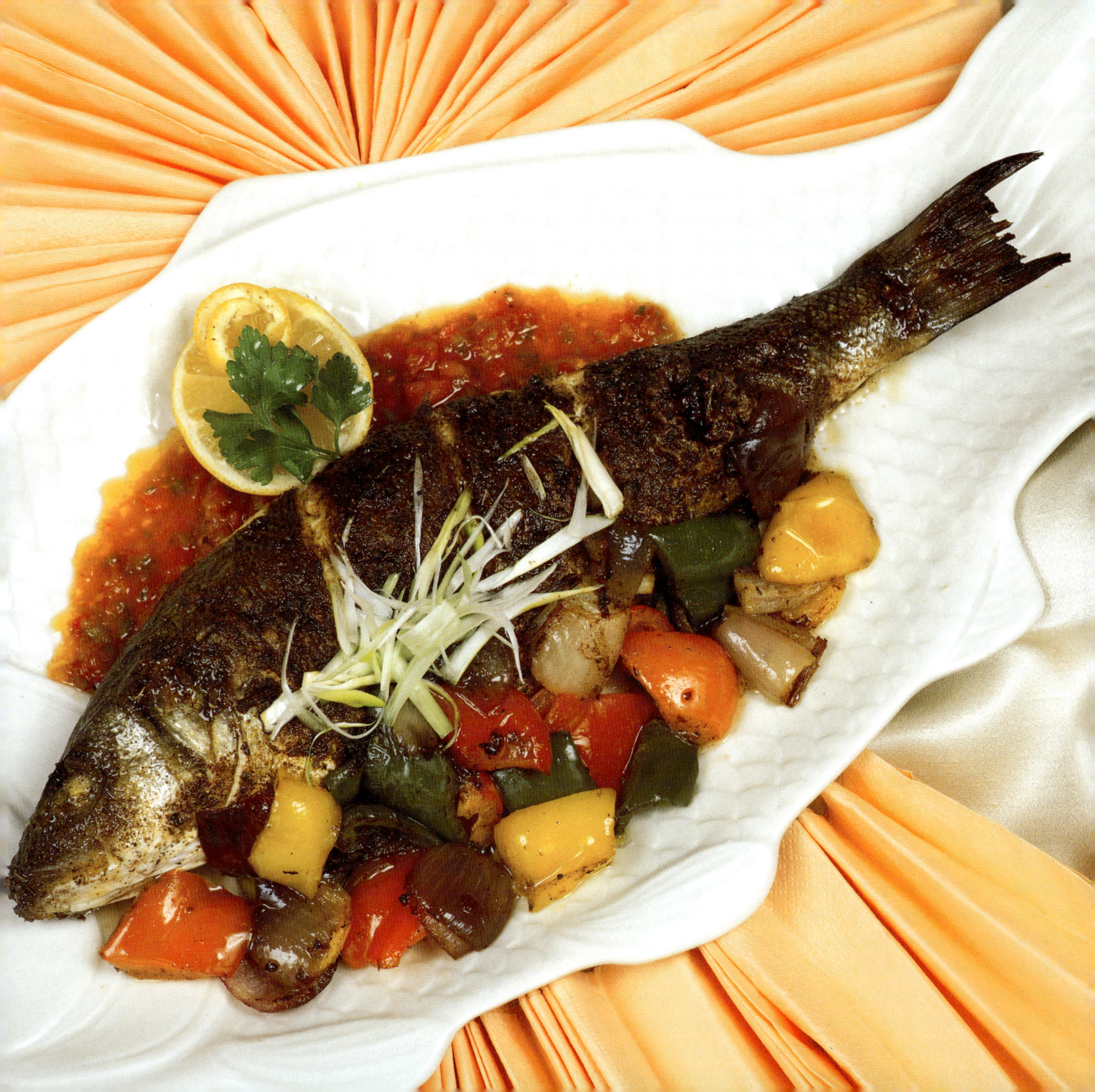

Honey Baked Breast of Duckling with Glazed Apples and Cider Sauce

The important thing to remember when cooking duck breasts, is to allow them time to rest once you take them out of the oven. Fresh from the oven, they are very active inside, and by carving immediately all their juices come flooding out. Give them five or six minutes to rest before slicing, then all their juices will stay where they belong, inside.

THIS IS WHAT YOU NEED
SERVES 4

4 FRESH DUCK BREASTS 6-7 OZ EACH.
2 APPLES ONE RED ONE GREEN, CORED AND CUT INTO EIGHT.
2 OZ SOFT BROWN SUGAR.
4 FL OZ DRY CIDER.
10 FL OZ JUS-LIE.*
1 FL OZ RASPBERRY WINE VINEGAR.
2 DESSERT SPOONS OF CLEAR HONEY.

*See "To Help You on Your Way" section

THIS IS WHAT YOU DO

Lay the duck breasts in a wide shallow pan, pour the honey over each of them nice and evenly and place them in a hot pre-heated oven for between twelve and fourteen minutes. There is no real need to season the duck breasts at this stage as the honey takes care of it all.

At the end of the cooking time, remove the breasts from the pan and set to one side to "rest". Now drain off the excess fat from the pan, leaving only the juices behind, place the pan onto a medium heat on the stove, get it sizzling then drop in the chunky pieces of apple. Stir them into the juices then sprinkle in the soft brown sugar, shake the pan to and fro, so the sugar will start to caramelise, allow it to attain a golden brown colour before pouring in the fruit vinegar.

Allow the vinegar to reduce or evaporate almost completely, then add the cider followed by the jus-lie, bring to the simmer, check the seasoning.

Slice the duck breasts, arrange onto plates, lift out the apples which should still have a "bite" to them and arrange them on the slices of duck. Strain the sauce over and serve.

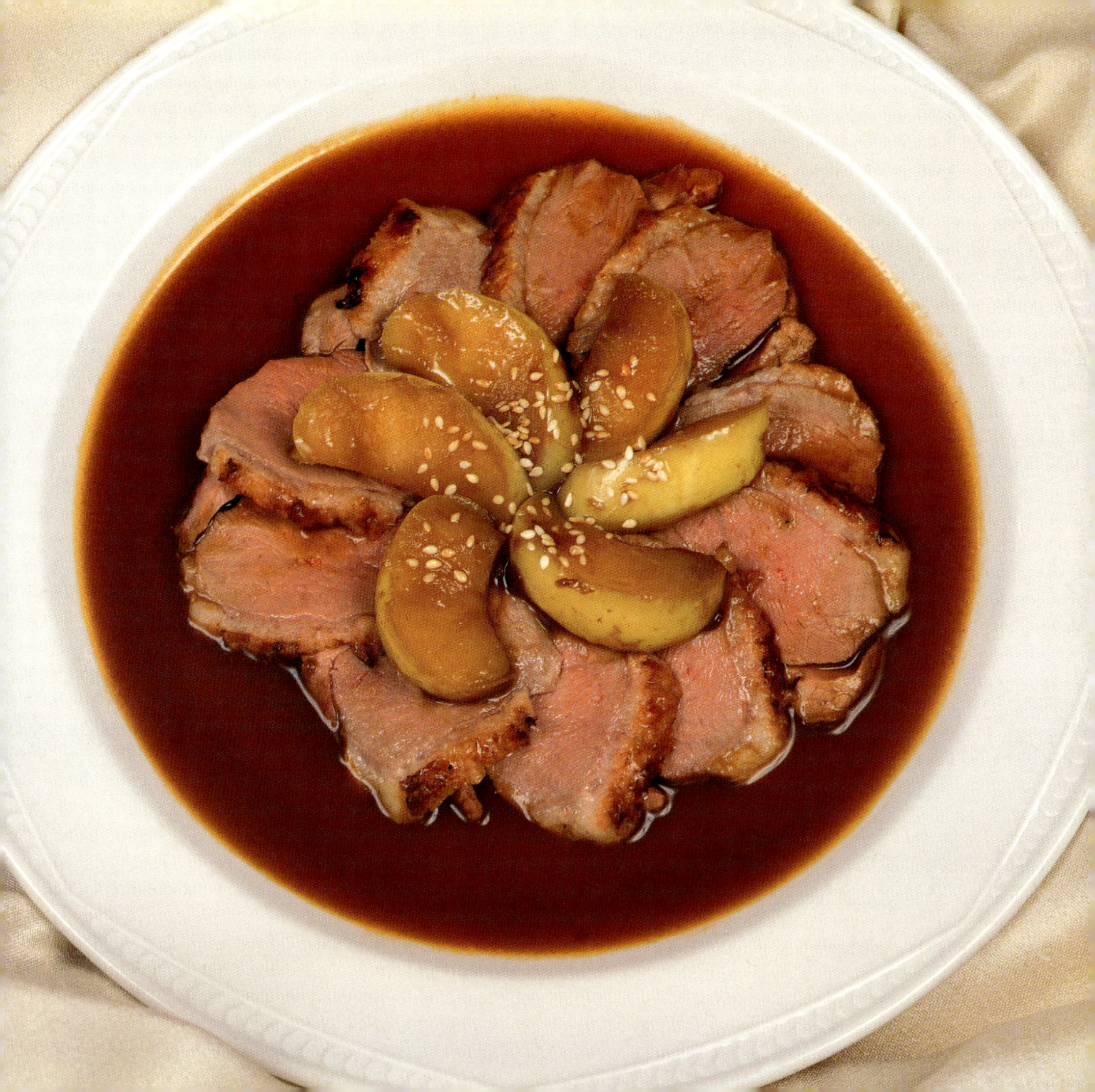

Saute of Beef in a Mustard and Pepper Sauce with Paprika Croutons

THIS IS WHAT YOU NEED
SERVES 4

1½ POUNDS OF DICED TOP SIDE OF BEEF (LARGE DICE).

6 OZ CHOPPED ONIONS.

2 CLOVES OF CRUSHED GARLIC.

2 ROUNDED TEASPOONS CRACKED BLACK PEPPER CORNS.

2 MEDIUM SIZED TOMATOES CHOPPED.

2 FL OZ WHITE WINE VINEGAR.

4 FL OZ DRY WHITE WINE.

15 FL OZ BEEF STOCK.

3 TEASPOONS OF GRAINY MUSTARD.

2 TEASPOONS OF GREEN PEPPER CORN MUSTARD.

4 OZ QUARTERED BUTTON MUSHROOMS, LIGHTLY SAUTEED.

10 FL OZ WHIPPING CREAM.

1 TEASPOON SOFT GREEN PEPPER CORNS.

SEASONING TO TASTE.

LITTLE OIL FOR COOKING.

THIS IS WHAT YOU DO

Heat a little oil in a thick bottomed casserole, season the diced beef with a sprinkle of salt, add to the pan, stir well to ensure that each piece of meat is sealed all over, keeping the pan good and hot. Add the vinegar, allow to evaporate before adding the onions and garlic. Once they begin to soften and colour a little, add the wine, chopped tomatoes and the cracked pepper corns. Stir well over a high flame so the tomatoes really break down into the other ingredients.

Add the mustards and the stock, bring to the boil, check the seasoning, then cover and place into a medium oven for 45 minutes. Lift out the beef from the casserole and set to one side. Pour in the cream, set the sauce to reduce down to the desired consistency, return the beef back to the pan, add the mushrooms and the green pepper corns and serve.

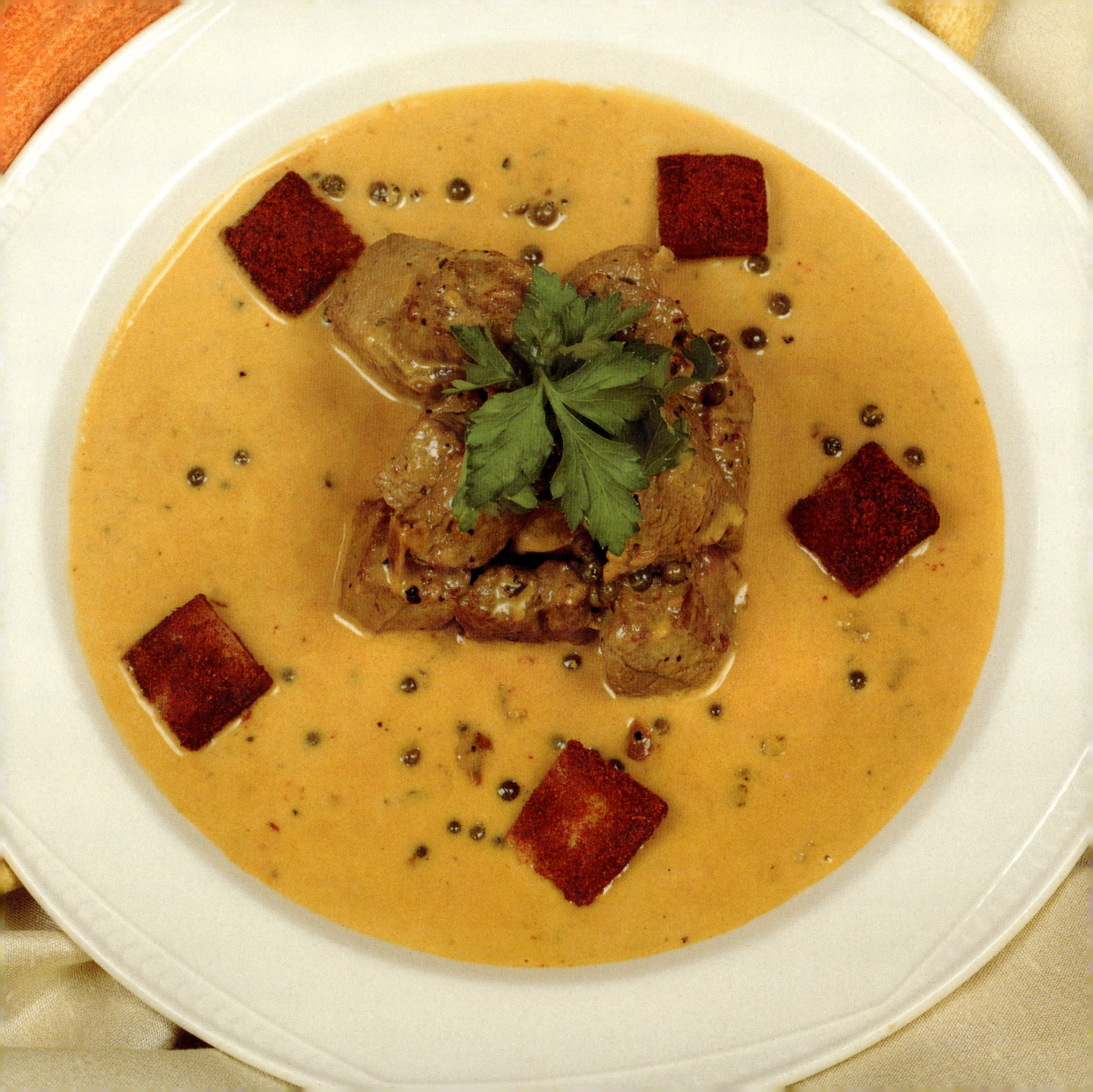

Welsh Lamb with Cracked Pepper and Fresh Blueberries

This is fast becoming something of a signature dish, it is so popular that people are ringing the bistro to check that it is still on the menu.

THIS IS WHAT YOU NEED
SERVES 4

4 SIX TO SEVEN OUNCE WELSH LEG OF LAMB STEAKS.
4 OZ CHOPPED ONIONS.
1 CLOVE OF CRUSHED GARLIC.
2 FL OZ RASPBERRY WINE VINEGAR.
1 LEVEL TEASPOON OF CRACKED BLACK PEPPERCORNS.
4 FL OZ FRESH ORANGE JUICE.
4 HEAPED TEASPOONS OF RED CURRANT JELLY.
5 FL OZ DRY WHITE WINE.
4 HEAPED TEASPOON TOMATO PUREE.
THREE QUARTERS OF A PINT OF WATER.
2 TEASPOONS OF HOI-SIN SAUCE.
3 TEASPOONS OF PLUM SAUCE.
4 OZ FRESH BLUEBERRIES.
LITTLE OIL FOR COOKING.
LITTLE BLANCHED ORANGE ZEST.
SALT AND PEPPER.

THIS IS WHAT YOU DO

Heat a little oil in an oven proof dish, season the lamb steaks and seal them in the hot oil on both sides. Add the onions and the garlic, keep them moving around the pan so that they soften and colour a little. Sprinkle in the cracked pepper corns, then the raspberry vinegar, allow this to reduce almost completely before adding the fresh orange juice, the red currant jelly and the wine.

Stir in the tomato puree, hoi-sin and the plum sauce together with half of the fresh blueberries, have all this simmering nicely, then pour in the water. Return to the simmer season, cover and place in a hot oven for about 45 minutes.

Lift out the lamb steaks and keep warm, then reduce the liquid down to a light sauce texture. Place each lamb steak onto a plate. Just before you serve the sauce check the seasoning, add the remaining fresh blueberries, and just as they are ready to "pop", pour the sauce over the lamb, finish with a little blanched orange zest and some crispy fried onions.*

*See "To Help You on Your Way" section

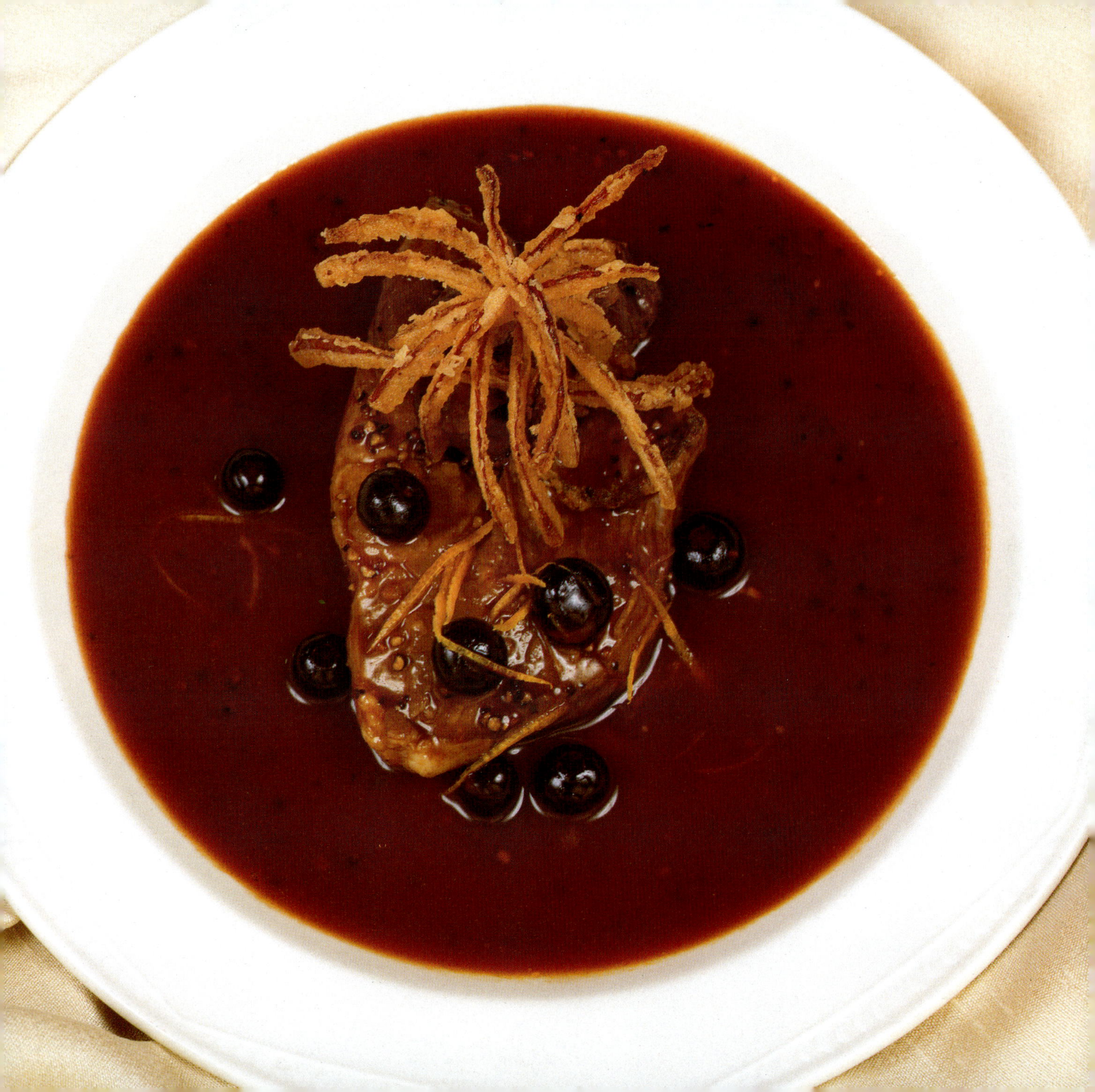

Roast Pheasant with Apple and Herb Dumplings on a Piquant Orange & Red Currant Sauce

This is always near the top of my ten best sellers list during the festive season. When fresh pheasants are no longer available, I give the same treatment to fresh guinea fowl.

THIS IS WHAT YOU NEED
SERVES 2.

1 FRESH PHEASANT (APPROX. 1LB 14 OZ).
SALT AND PEPPER.
2 FL OZ RED WINE VINEGAR.
SPRINKLE OF CRACKED BLACK PEPPERCORNS.
2 TEASPOONS OF RED CURRANT JELLY.
10 FL OZ JUS-LIE.*
4 FL OZ FRESH ORANGE JUICE.
COOKING OIL.

THIS IS WHAT YOU DO

Use a small roasting tray or saute pan, one that the bird just fits nicely into. Heat a little of the oil in the pan, season the bird inside and out, then carefully brown it all over in the hot oil. Set the bird to rest on its back, in the pan (breast up), and cook in a medium hot oven for about 35-40 minutes, basting frequently.

Once the pheasant is cooked, lift it out and put to one side to rest. Drain off the excess fat from the pan, pour in the red wine vinegar, reduce almost entirely before adding the orange juice, red currant jelly and a light sprinkle of cracked black pepper corns. Reduce all this by half then pour in the jus-lie, simmer, reduce and check the seasoning.

Remove the breasts and legs from the pheasant and lay one of each onto two warm main course plates. Strain the sauce and pour around the portions, garnish with a couple of orange segments, and as many as you like of the apple and herb dumplings.*

*See "To Help You on Your Way" section

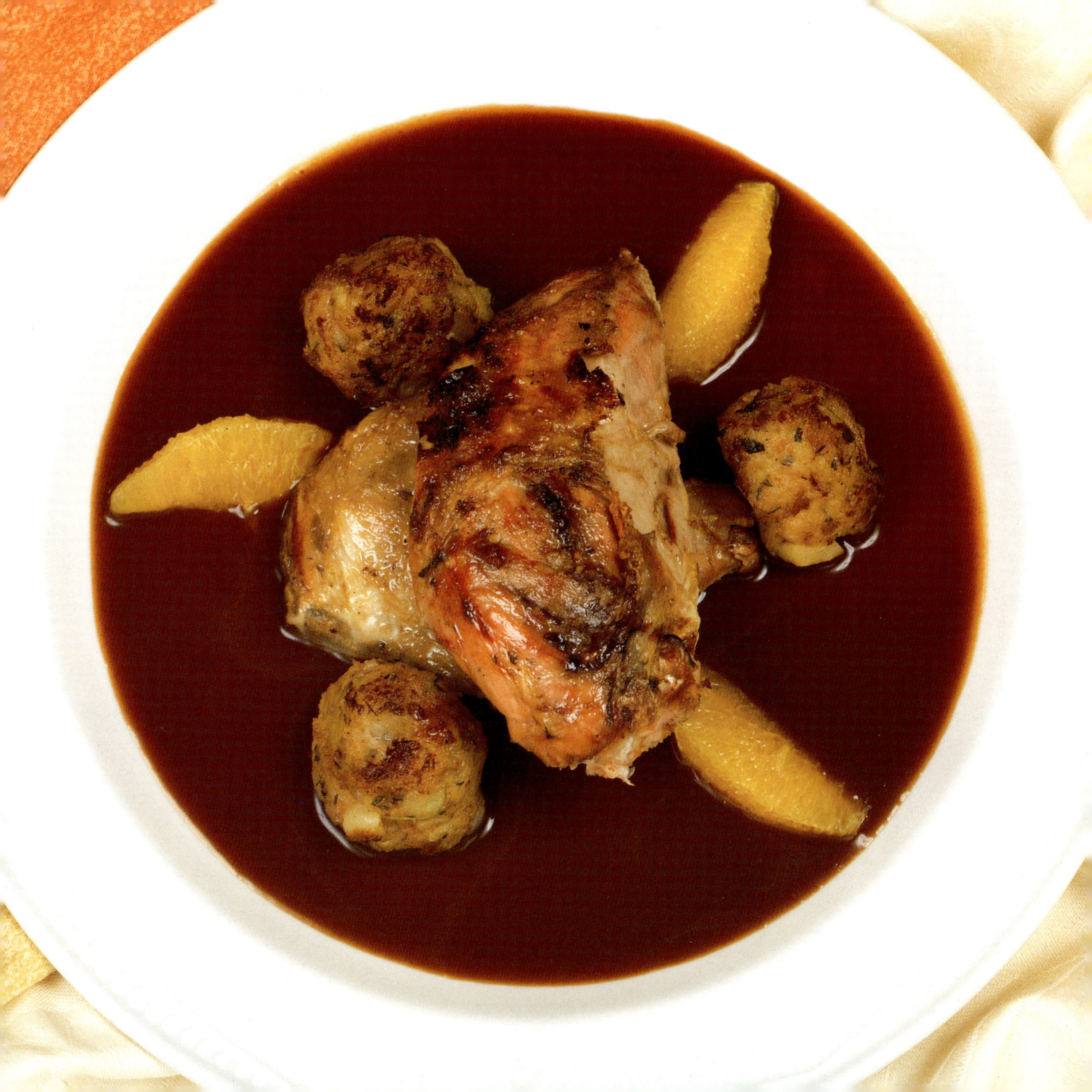

Pencarreg and Vegetable Filo's with a Baked Tomato Dressing

Eating out should be a pleasure for everyone, for vegetarians though, it can sometimes be a nightmare. The only limit to how creative you can be when cooking with vegetable dishes, is your own imagination. What's more you do not have to be vegetarian to enjoy this dish.

THIS IS WHAT YOU NEED
SERVES 4.

LITTLE OLIVE OIL FOR COOKING.
2 OZ CHOPPED ONIONS.
4 OZ COURGETTES, QUARTERED LENGTHWAYS AND SLICED.
2 OZ SLICED BUTTON MUSHROOMS.
2 OZ DICED RED PEPPER.
2 OZ DICED GREEN PEPPER.
1 SMALL CLOVE OF CRUSHED GARLIC.
2 OZ BLANCHED ASPARAGUS, 3 GOOD SIZED SPEARS, SLICED.
2 FL OZ DRY WHITE WINE.
1 OZ FIRM BUTTER.
4 FULL SHEETS OF FILO PASTRY CUT IN HALF.
2 OZ MELTED BUTTER.
8 OZ COOKED BASMATI RICE, COLOURED WITH A LITTLE TURMERIC.
4 OZ PIECE OF PENCARREG CHEESE, CUT INTO FOUR CHUNKY PIECES.
SALT AND PEPPER.

*See "To Help You on Your Way" section

THIS IS WHAT YOU DO

Heat a little olive oil in a sturdy frying pan, cook the onions, garlic, peppers, mushrooms and the courgettes together in the hot oil until they just begin to soften. Stir in the cooked asparagus and rice, season with salt and pepper, then moisten the ingredients with the dash of dry white wine, mix well. Break the 1oz of firm butter into smaller pieces and stir into the rice mixture, checking the seasoning as you go. Leave to one side to cool.

Now lay one half sheet of pastry onto the work top, brush lightly with the melted butter, lay another half sheet on top at an angle so there are eight corners, brush this sheet as you did the previous one. Spoon an amount of the rice mixture in the centre, place a piece of the cheese in the middle then cover with some more of the rice. Fold each side of the pastry over the rice, then tuck the ends underneath. Repeat this process until all four are done. Place on a lightly buttered baking sheet, brush the tops with a little butter, sprinkle with a few poppy seeds and bake in a medium oven until nice and golden. Serve with the delicious baked tomato dressing.*

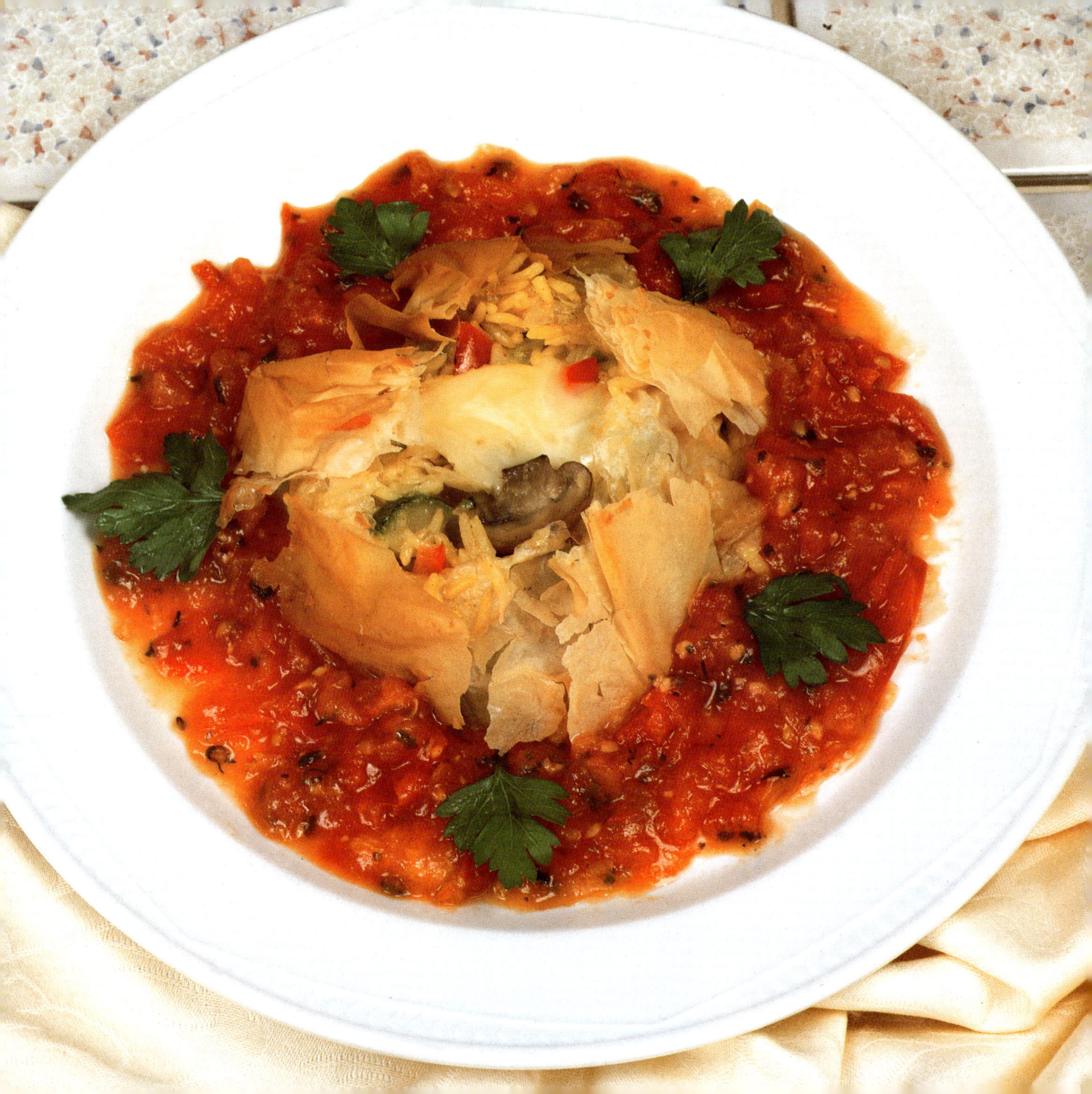

Caramelised Red Onion Tart

This makes a very tasty lunch or snack, you can caramelise any onions but I find the large spanish or these red onions the sweetest.

THIS IS WHAT YOU NEED

1LB PUFF PASTRY.
1LB THINLY SLICED RED ONIONS.
2 LARGE CRUSHED CLOVES OF GARLIC.
3 LEVEL TEASPOONS OF HOI-SIN.
2 OZ GRATED CHEDDAR CHEESE.
SPRINKLE OF MIXED HERBS.
LITTLE SALT AND PEPPER.
LITTLE OLIVE OIL FOR COOKING.

THIS IS WHAT YOU DO

Use a thick bottomed non-stick frying pan, heat a little olive oil, just enough to coat the base of the pan, add the sliced red onions, give them a good stir so that they are well mixed with the oil. Add the crushed garlic and leave them cook gently on the stove over a medium heat.

This could take between 12 and 15 minutes, but slowly the onions will soften and release their natural sugars and become syrupy and delicious. Add a small sprinkle of mixed herbs, then the hoi-sin check the seasoning then leave to one side.

Roll out the puff pastry, so its about a quarter of an inch thick, using a saucer cut out 4 pastry discs.

Lay the pastries on a baking sheet, spread the caramelised onions on top of each leaving a half inch rim around the edge clear. Top this with the grated cheddar cheese, then bake in a hot oven until well risen and golden brown.

Serve with a crisp well dressed salad . Since the picture was taken I have started putting a two ounce slice of mild goats cheese on top instead of the cheddar, its worth trying.

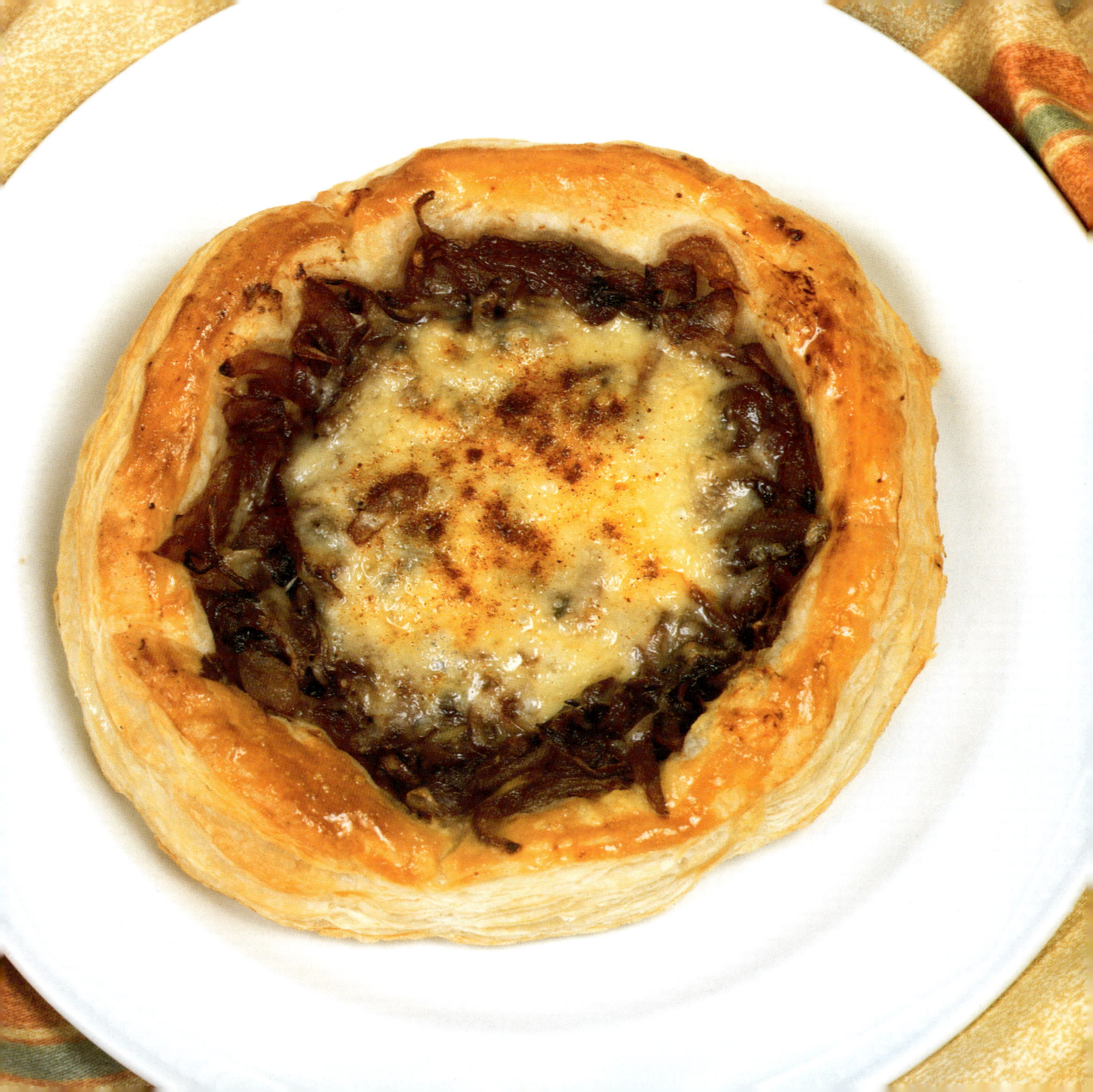

The Gower Peninsula

My childhood was spent living with my family in Dunvant, a village that forms a gateway to the Gower. I remember cycling and walking along many of the roads and lanes on the peninsula, as I made my way with friends to our favourite places, taking for granted the unspoilt wonder of the place. The fact that the Gower Peninsula was Britain's First designated Area of Outstanding Beauty was not particularly important to us, after all this was simply our play area, with something new to discover every day.

Years later, when returning home after working in London, there were still more discoveries. I became spellbound at the range and quality of fresh local produce coming from The Gower, I really had no idea that such a food store was present on my own door step.

Leeks, potatoes, cauliflowers, cabbage and swedes fill the stalls at Swansea Market, as do beans, carrots, tomatoes, beetroot and peas, all fresh from The Gower. Picking your own strawberries, raspberries and gooseberries together with fresh currants is a popular weekend pastime, attracting people from miles around.

A type of seaweed, which in my youth resembled shredded black bags clinging to the rocks, is Lavaweed, which is harvested from secret locations, often at night, which is washed then simmered for several hours and minced to become Laverbread .

Before the tractors came

During the summer months, fresh crab, lobster and seabass would battle for supremacy, on menus and shopping lists.

Discovering all this for the first time, as well as Gower beef and lamb, especially lamb off the salt marshes on the north coast, just filled me with a sense of pride.

These days, I take none of this for granted, I cherish the Gower, as do many Chefs, for Gower is a very special natural food store.

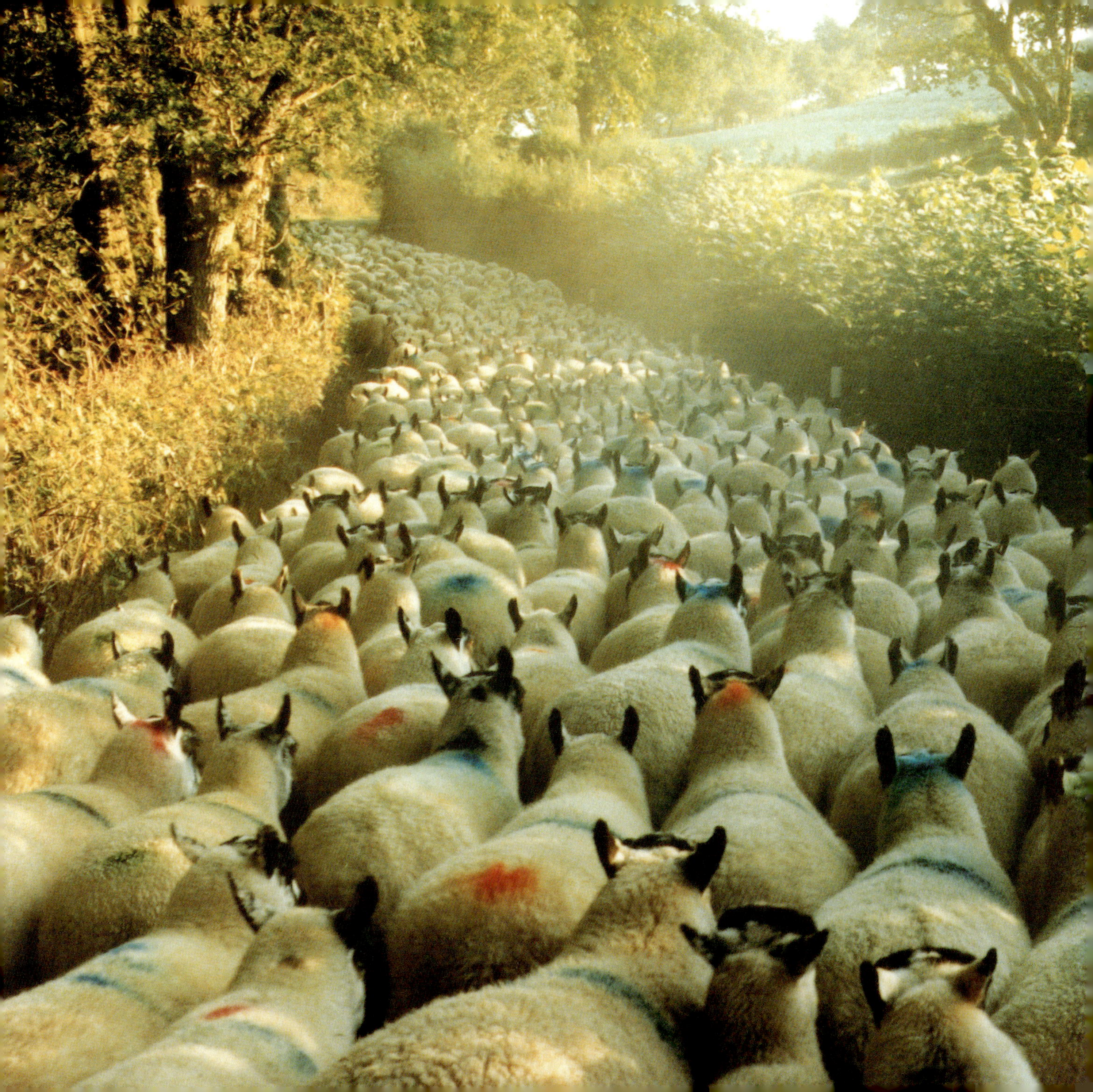

to Finish

And there a sweet girl stood and spread
The table with good things,
Felinfoel beer with a mountain's head,
And a pheasant with hungry wings.

Vernon Watkins
(from 'Ballad of the Mari Lwyd' 1941)

Hot Caramelised Pear Tart and Butterscotch Sauce

This really is as simple as can be, but never the less a very popular dessert, it's probably the butter scotch sauce that makes the difference, but it's also excellent with ice cream.

THIS IS WHAT YOU NEED
SERVES 4.

1LB PUFF PASTRY.
2 FIRM DESSERT PEARS.
2 OZ BROWN SUGAR.

THIS IS WHAT YOU DO

Roll out the pastry so its ¼ inch thick. Cut out four five inch discs, and lay them onto a baking sheet.

Quarter the pears, cut out the core and slice thinly. Arrange on top of each pastry in a circular formation, sprinkle with a little brown sugar and bake in a hot oven until golden brown and well risen.

BUTTERSCOTCH SAUCE

THIS IS WHAT YOU NEED

4 OZ BROWN SUGAR.
2 OZ BUTTER.
½ PINT OF WHIPPING CREAM.

THIS IS WHAT YOU DO

Melt the butter in a thick bottomed pan, add the sugar and stir over a medium heat.

Slowly at first, the butter and the sugar will caramelise, allow it to reach a dark golden colour, before pouring in the whipping cream.

Bring the pan to the boil, still stirring so that the caramel dissolves into the cream.

Pour the sauce into a jug to cool.

This can be served hot or cold.

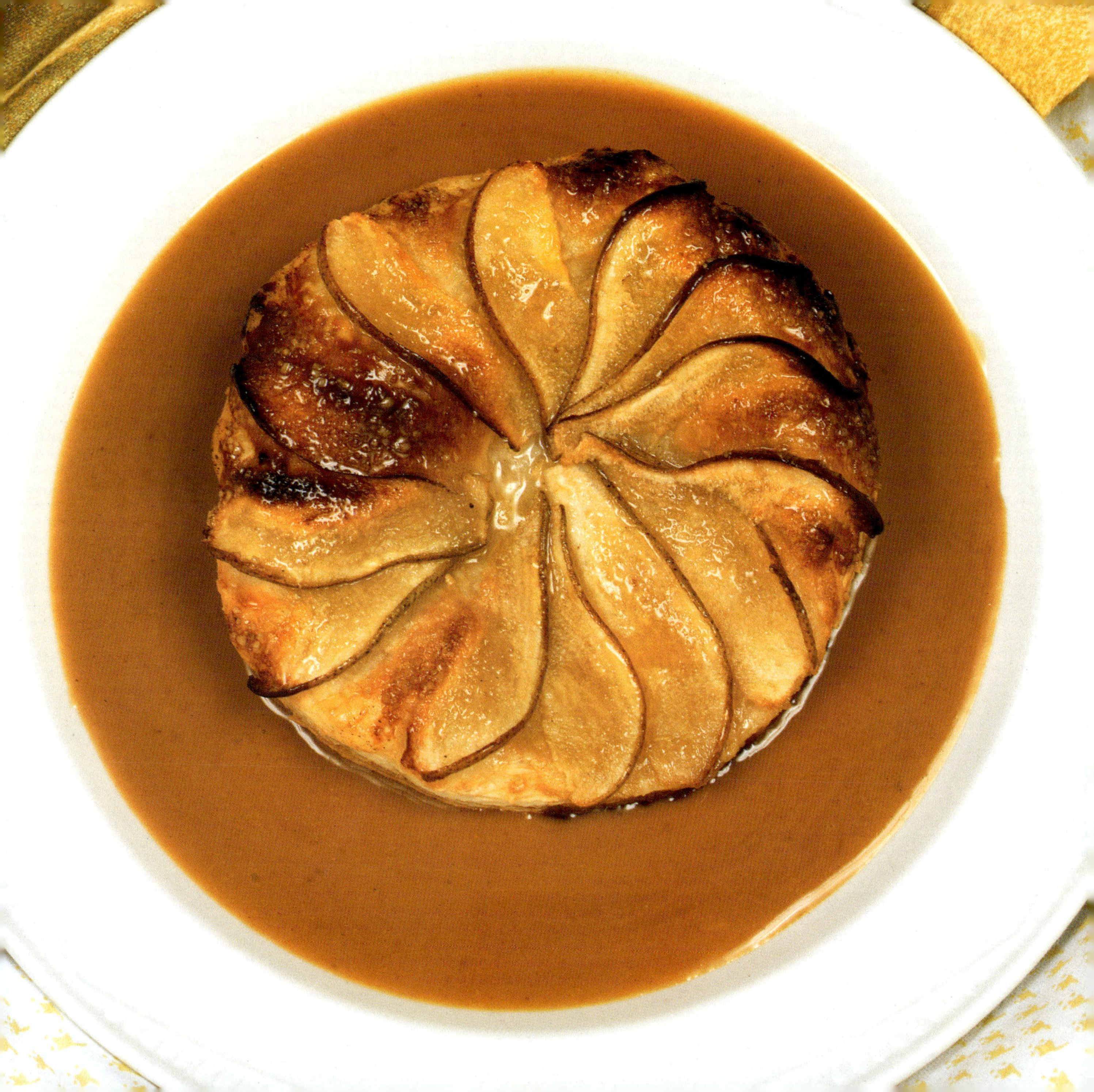

Mousse of White Chocolate on a Dark Chocolate Sauce

As a confirmed chocoholic, I couldn't eat too much of this one, eaten separately the dark chocolate, white chocolate and the oranges are lovely, but together on your spoon, they are unbelievable!

THIS IS WHAT YOU NEED
SERVES 6-8 (normal portions)

1PT WHIPPING CREAM.
1LB WHITE CHOCOLATE.
5 LEAVES OF GELATINE.

THIS IS WHAT YOU DO

Melt the chocolate in a small pan, that is sitting on top of a larger pan of boiling water.

Whip the cream lightly until it forms soft peaks.

Fold the melted white chocolate into the cream.

Break the gelatine leaves into the small pan that the chocolate was melted in, and add 2 fl oz of water, bring to the boil while stirring until it dissolves.

Strain the dissolved gelatine into the cream and chocolate mixture, stir in gently.

Pour into a container, cover and place in the fridge until set.

Using two dessert spoons, shape into little ovals (quenelles), and set upon a pool of the dark chocolate sauce, garnish with oranges sitting in a little russe biscuit.

FOR THE SAUCE
THIS IS WHAT YOU NEED

2 OZ DARK CHOCOLATE.
5 FL OZ WHIPPING CREAM.
2 FL OZ ORANGE JUICE.

THIS IS WHAT YOU DO

Melt the chocolate in a small pan, that is sitting on top of a larger pan of boiling water.

Bring the cream to the boil and mix it into the chocolate, add the orange juice. At this stage you could if you wish add a dash of your favourite liqueur or spirit.

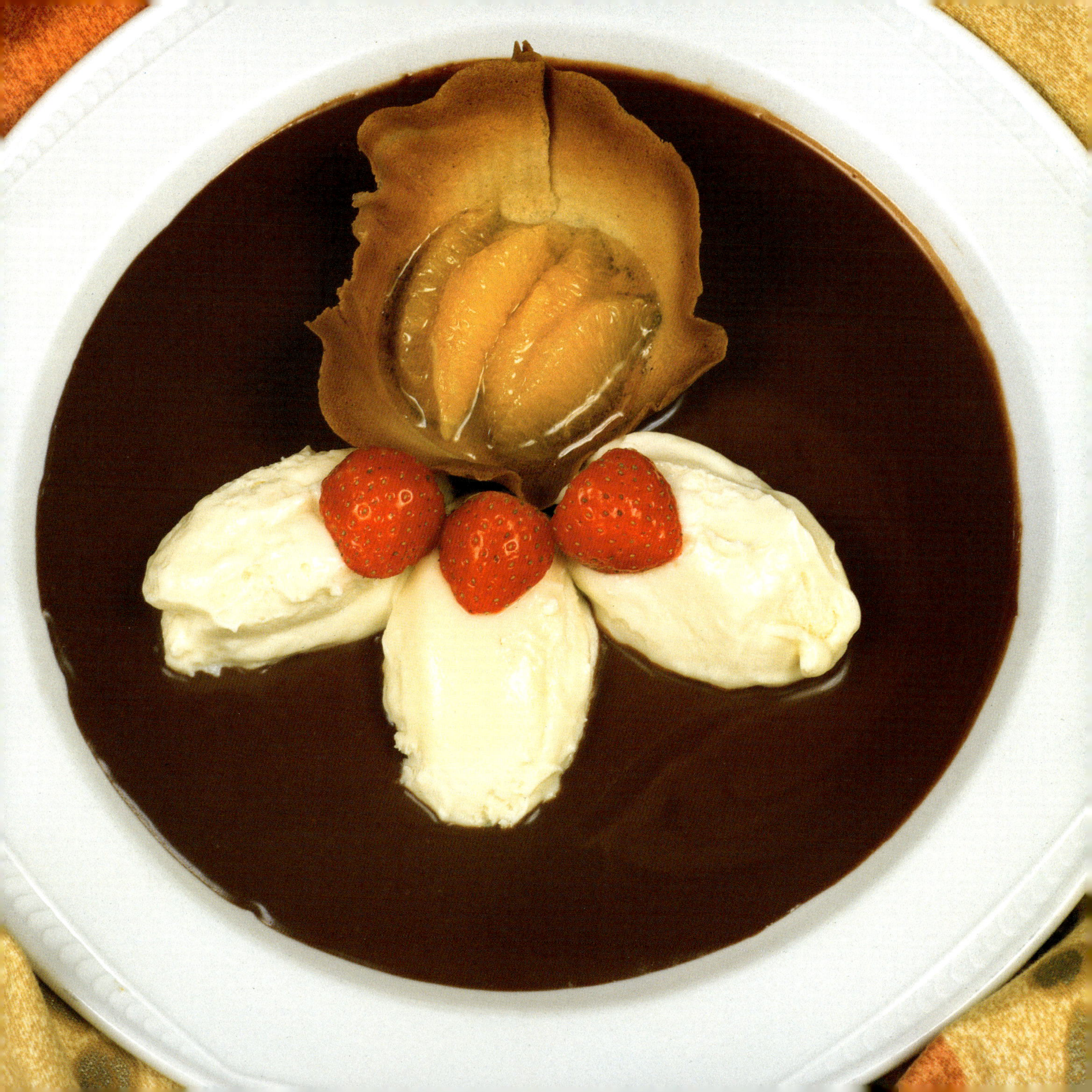

Russe Biscuit with Fresh Fruit

**THIS IS WHAT YOU NEED
SERVES 6.**

2 OZ PLAIN FLOUR, SIFTED.
2 OZ MELTED BUTTER, JUST WARM.
2 OZ CASTER SUGAR.
2 EGG WHITES.
FRESH FRUIT OF YOUR CHOICE.

THIS IS WHAT YOU DO

Firstly, beat the egg whites and the sugar together to form stiff peaks, carefully fold in the sifted plain flour, then slowly incorporate the warm melted butter.

The result is a smooth, glossy paste, now prepare a very lightly buttered baking tray, a non stick one would be a good idea, apply some of the mixture to the centre of the tray, then with a palette knife gently spread it out with a circular motion, into a five or six inch disc, about as thin as you can make it without it being see through.

Before it goes into the oven, make sure you have ready a jam or honey jar, a clean palette knife and a tea towel, now the tray can go into the hot oven.

Depending on your particular oven, cooking will take anything between 6 and 10 minutes.

Keep your eye on it, then just as it becomes a light golden brown, remove from the oven. Now with one hand, slide the palette knife underneath it, lift gently onto the open tea towel in your other hand. Put the knife down, and press the bottom of the jam jar into the centre of the biscuit. Still holding the towel with one hand and the jar in the other, with the biscuit in between, invert it so that the jar is underneath and the towel is on top, and of course the biscuit is still in place.

When cool, give the jam jar a gentle quarter twist, to free it from the biscuit, turn everything back over, remove the jar then carefully separate the biscuit from the tea towel.

From the moment you remove the tray from the oven, the biscuit is cooling, when it cools it turns, nice and crisp, so the shaping process has to be done very quickly indeed.

It may sound a little difficult, and you will probably need a few dummy runs at it, but once you get the hang of it, its a piece of cake.

Fill with whipped cream and seasonal berries. Serve on a Red Fruit Coulis.*

*See "To Help You on Your Way" section

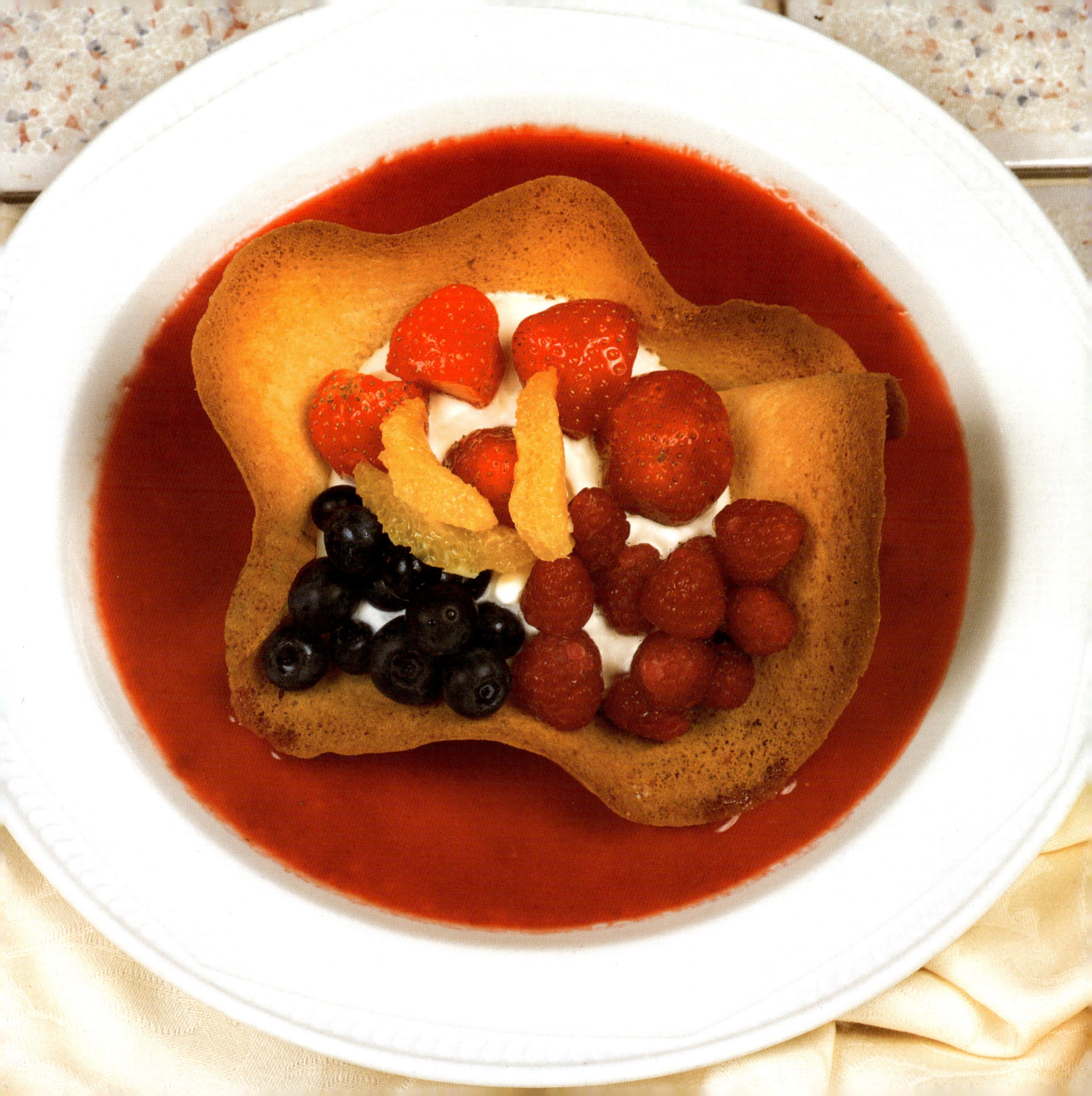

Bread and Butter Pudding

One of my fondest memories as a child, is my mum's bread and butter pudding, and it still remains my dad's favourite. It was never quite as rich as this one, but it was special.

THIS IS WHAT YOU NEED
SERVES 6-8

10 BUTTERED SLICES OF FRESH BREAD, MEDIUM THICK.
12 WHOLE EGGS.
¾ PT MILK.
¾ PT WHIPPING CREAM.
GOOD DASH OF VANILLA.
6 OZ WHITE SUGAR.
LITTLE BROWN SUGAR FOR GLAZING.
6 OZ PLUMP SULTANAS.
2 OZ CHOPPED PECAN NUTS.

THIS IS WHAT YOU DO

Lay the slices of buttered bread, in single layers, with a generous sprinkle of sultanas between each, in a large baking dish.

Beat the eggs and the sugar together until they are well mixed then add the milk and cream followed by the vanilla.

Pour the custard slowly over the bread, pressing down gently, forcing the bread down into the milk and cream mixture.

Sprinkle with brown sugar and chopped pecan nuts, bake in a medium hot oven for about 45 minutes.

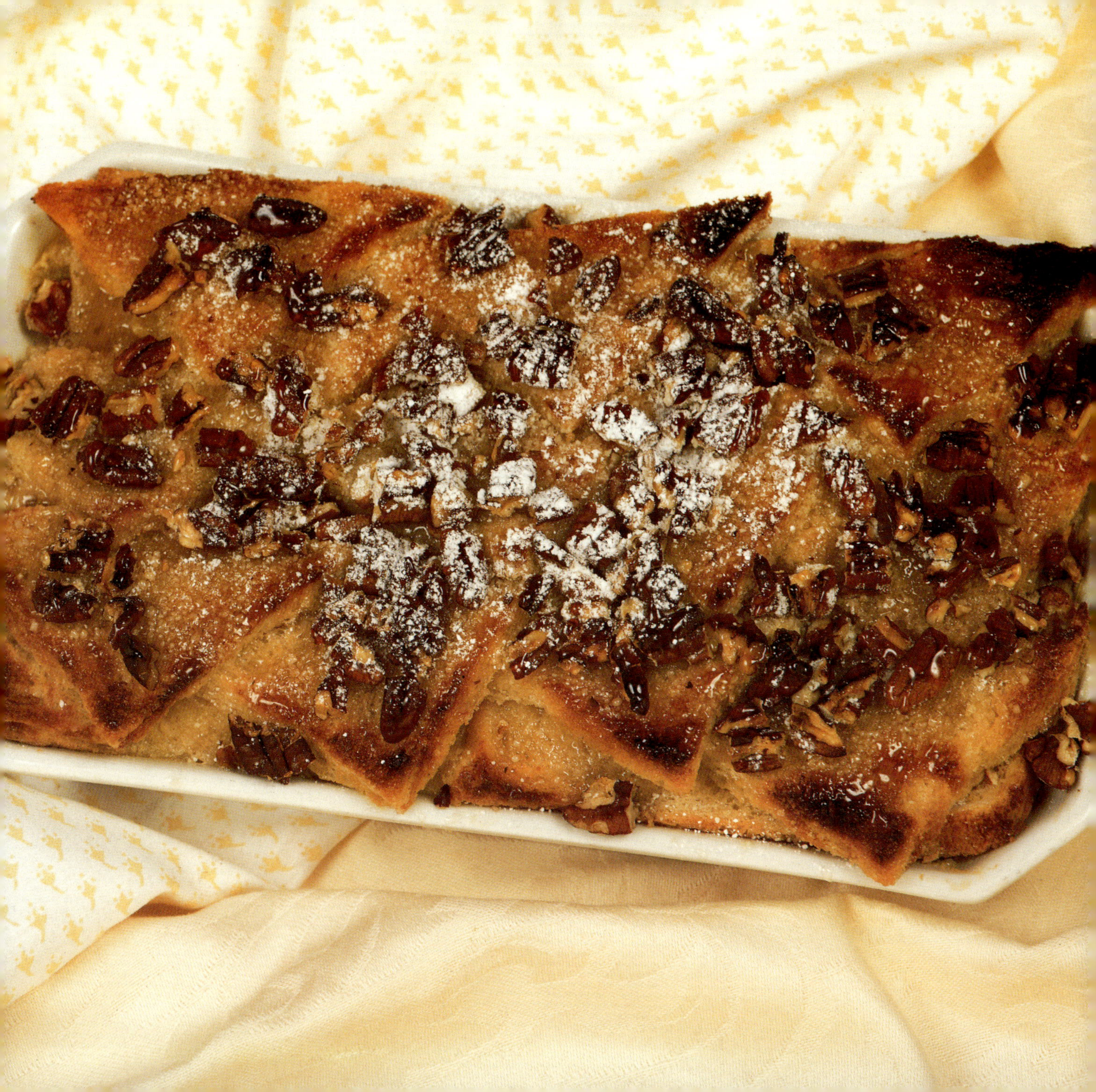

Seasonal Fruit Crumble

THIS IS WHAT YOU NEED

12 OZ SLICED APPLE, CORED AND SKINNED.
12 OZ SLICED PEAR, CORED AND SKINNED.
8 OZ DARK PLUMS, SEGMENTED.
8 OZ STRAWBERRIES, QUARTERED.
4 OZ RASPBERRIES.
4 OZ BLUEBERRIES.
4 OZ MELTED BUTTER.
4 OZ GRANULATED SUGAR.
5 FL OZ FRESH ORANGE JUICE.
2 LEVEL TEASPOONS, MIXED SPICE.

THIS IS WHAT YOU DO

Heat the butter until sizzling in a large pan, add the apples and pears, stir into the butter, and cook for a few minutes, just as they start to soften add the plums, sugar, orange juice and the mixed spice, stir gently so not to break the fruit up too much.

The juices from the fruit, will mix with the sugar and orange juice and thicken into a delicious sauce in next to no time.

Check that the sweetness is to your liking, then stir in the berries. Pour the mixture into a suitable dish, top with the crumble and bake in a medium oven for about 35 minutes. Just before the cooking time is complete sprinkle lightly with brown sugar, this makes a lovely glaze.

FOR THE CRUMBLE

THIS IS WHAT YOU NEED

8 OZ PLAIN FLOUR.
4 OZ BROWN SUGAR.
2 OZ DESICCATED COCONUT.
3 OZ FIRM BUTTER.

THIS IS WHAT YOU DO

Put the flour, sugar and coconut into a food processor, give it a good whizz, until all is well mixed, then add the firm butter cut up into small pieces and mix to a crumbly texture.

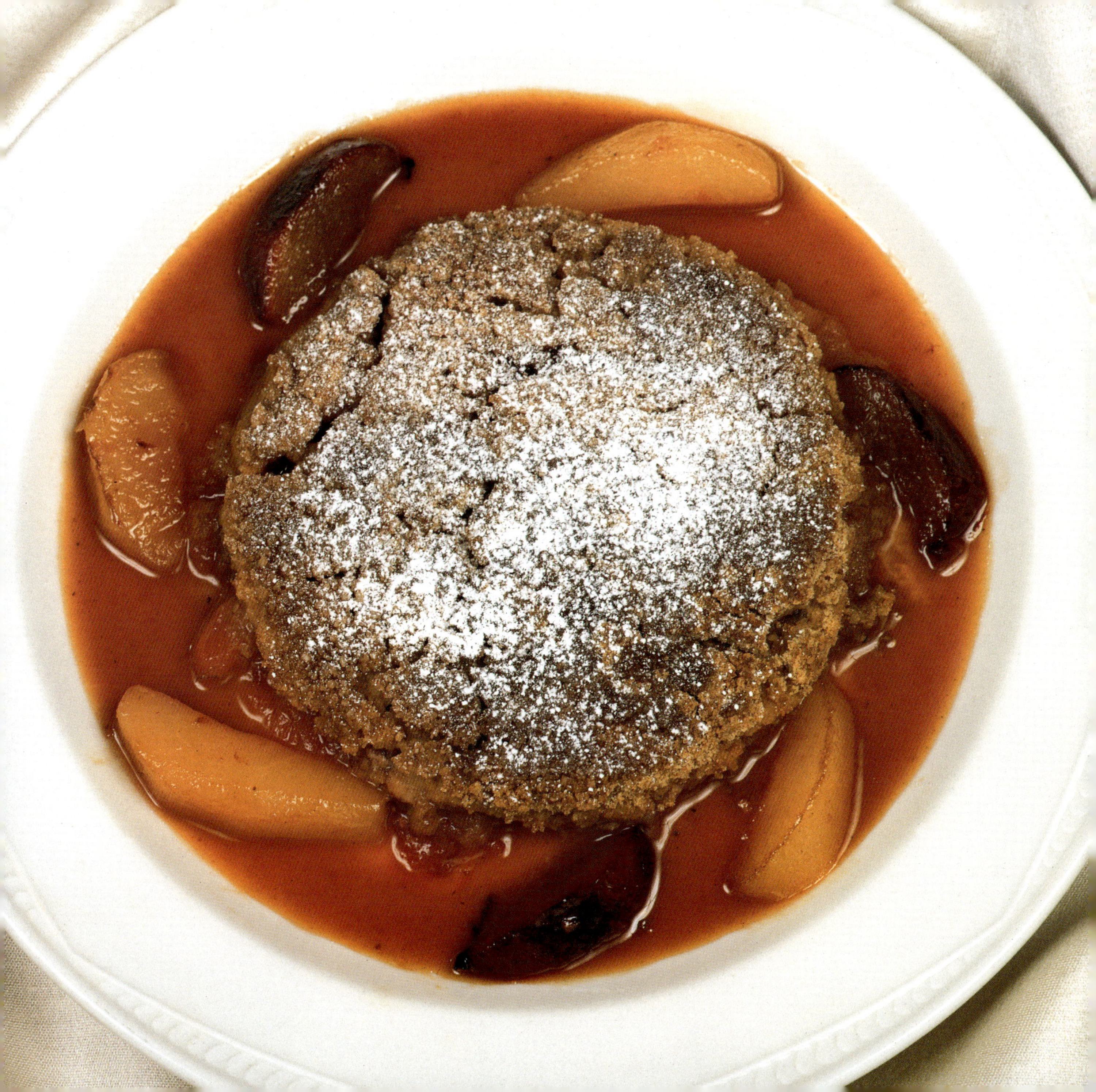

Some of Our Greatest Products, Welsh Cheeses

Soft organic Pencarreg, full flavoured Llanboidy and Gouda style Tiefi. Just three of my favourites from a growing number of superb Welsh Cheeses.

To Help You on Your Way

MUSTARD AND HERB CRUMBLE

2 OZ BUTTER.
2 OZ CHOPPED ONION.
4 OZ FRESH BREADCRUMBS.
SPRINKLE OF MIXED HERBS.
SALT AND PEPPER.
1 TEASPOON GRAINY MUSTARD.

Melt the butter in a shallow frying pan, once sizzling add the onions and cook gently, until softened, add the crumbs, mustard and mixed herbs, stir and mix well. Continue to cook whilst stirring until the crumbs become crisp and dry, season and use as required. Add two teaspoons of soft green peppercorns for use with the mussels.

SWEET PEPPER SALSA

2 RED PEPPERS.
4 OZ ONIONS.
2 LARGE CLOVES OF GARLIC.
12 OZ RIPE TOMATOES.
7 FL OZ EXTRA VIRGIN OLIVE OIL.
5 FL OZ TOMATO KETCHUP.
SALT AND PEPPER.

Have all ingredients prepared for use, then place all into a food processor, and blend to form a delicious sauce. This recipe makes, one and a half pints.

APPLE AND HERB DUMPLINGS

4 OZ FRESH BREADCRUMBS.
1 OZ BUTTER.
1 OZ CHOPPED SHALLOTS.
1 DESSERT APPLE, PEELED AND FINELY CHOPPED.
SPRINKLE OF MIXED HERBS.
2 FL OZ DRY CIDER.
2 TEASPOONS OF PLUM SAUCE.
LITTLE SEASONING.

Melt the butter, add the shallots and cook gently until softened, add the chopped apple and mix well.

Stir in the bread crumbs and mixed herbs, then the cider and plum sauce, season and allow to cool. Divide the mixture into equal portions and roll into dumpling shapes. Place onto a baking tray brush with a little butter, then grill or roast until golden brown, serve with the pheasant dish.

CRISPY FRIED LEEKS

Trim and cut the leek in half lengthways, slice it finely across to form semi-circles.

Wash, then dip them into seasoned flour, shake off any excess, and deep fry until crisp and golden. This also works well with finely slices onions. Best served as soon as ready.

JUS-LIE

A Jus-Lie, is simply a lightly thickened stock. I offer two stocks here, one traditional, the other far more convenient. It works well with any recipe in this book that asks for "Jus-Lie", and is very popular with everyone at my "Food and Cookery Theatre".

BASIC RED WINE AND VEGETABLE STOCK

4 OZ MINCED OR FINELY CHOPPED CARROTS.
4 OZ MINCED OR FINELY CHOPPED ONIONS.
4 OZ MINCED OR FINELY CHOPPED CELERY.
4 OZ MINCED OR FINELY CHOPPED MUSHROOMS.
3 CRUSHED CLOVES OF GARLIC.
SPRINKLE OF MIXED HERBS.
5 FL OZ RED WINE.
1½ PINTS OF WATER
2 TEASPOONS OF HOI-SIN.
4 TEASPOONS OF TOMATO PUREE.
LITTLE OIL FOR COOKING.
SALT AND PEPPER.

Fry all the vegetables and garlic in a very small amount of oil. Keep stirring and allow them to turn golden brown. Pour in the red wine, reduce a little then add the water, herbs, Hoi-Sin and tomato puree. Simmer gently to reduce by at least one third. Season and use when required.

BASIC RED WINE STOCK

1LB BEEF BONES CHOPPED SMALL.
8 OZ LAMB BONES CHOPPED SMALL.
8 OZ ONIONS.
4 OZ CHOPPED CARROT.
4 OZ CHOPPED LEEKS.
4 OZ CHOPPED CELERY.
1 SMALL HEAD OF GARLIC CUT IN HALF.
LITTLE COOKING OIL.
4 OZ TOMATO PUREE.
SPRINKLE OF MIXED HERBS.

Place all the chopped bones and vegetables, together with the halved head of garlic onto a roasting tray. Rub in a little cooking oil, sprinkle with a little salt and roast in a hot oven, stirring frequently. Allow all to become well roasted, before placing in a pot, cover with 5 pints of cold water, bring to the boil, add the herbs and tomato puree, then set to simmer and reduce by half. Strain and use as required.

Each of these stocks will need a teaspoon of "Beurre Manie" stirred into them to thicken lightly before straining. Simply blend equal quantities of soft butter and plain flour to form a paste.

BAKED TOMATO DRESSING

6 SMALL RIPE TOMATOES.
2 OZ RED ONIONS.
1 LARGE CLOVE OF GARLIC.
A SPRINKLE OF MIXED HERBS.
A DRIBBLE OF OLIVE OIL.
SALT AND PEPPER.

Cut the tomatoes in half and the red onion into small chunks. Cut the garlic in half and place all onto a roasting tray, pour on a dribble of olive oil, a sprinkle of mixed herbs, then roast in a hot oven until all is nicely caramelised. Blend in a processor, season and serve.

Should you wish to lengthen or thin the sauce, simply add a little extra olive oil whilst in the processor.

RED FRUIT COULIS

Take 4 oz of strawberries and 2 oz of raspberries and place into a small pot. Cover with half orange juice, half water. Add a sprinkle of sugar to taste, poach the fruit and reduce to a rich red syrup. Strain, chill and serve.

LEMON AND GARLIC SAUCE

5 FL OZ WHIPPING CREAM.
½ CLOVE OF GARLIC.
PINCH OF TURMERIC.
GOOD SQUEEZE OF FRESH LEMON JUICE.
THE LIQUID FROM THE POACHED SALMON, AT LEAST 4 FL OZ.
DASH OF VERMOUTH.
SEASONING.

Set the fish stock to simmer with the garlic. Add the cream, turmeric and vermouth. Reduce gently to a light consistency, check the seasoning and finish with a little lemon juice. Strain and serve with the fishcakes on page 20.

PANCAKE BATTER

2 EGGS.
2 OZ PLAIN FLOUR.
8 FL OZ COLD WATER.
SPRINKLE OF MIXED HERBS.
LITTLE SALT AND PEPPER.
2 DESERT SPOONS OF OLIVE OIL.

Beat the eggs and gradually incorporate the sifted flour to form a smooth paste. Pour in all the cold water a little at a time. Add the herbs, seasoning and olive oil.

The Mumbles Lighthouse

Acknowledgments

We would like to thank the following people for their support, encouragement and contributions, which enabled us to blend together our ideas and cook up this book.

The City and Council of Swansea, also Swansea Museums Collections.
From "BARROWS" in Mumbles, Richard and Heather Horton and Darren Thomas.
Jeff Towns of Dylans Bookstore, Roger Tiley, Francis Green, Alyson, Brian and Hayley Jones.
Della Williams and Local Historian Carol Powell and her husband John of the Oystermouth Historical Association.

Viscase, The Framing Machine, Charlotte's Web Bookshop, The Fabric Mill, Fred Ley and Sons, Roger Thomas the Butchers, The Management of Sketty Hall, and everyone attending
Chris Keenan's Cookery Theatre, Andrew Forbes, Shaun and Glen of the Shaun Condron Partnership. Elizabeth Shapton, Peter and Jenny Venables.
Anthony Evans and Sarah Rees of DWJ Colourprint. J.M Dent Publisher and Trustees for the Copyright of Dylan Thomas, Mrs Vernon Watkins, and Sir Harry Secombe.

ISBN 0-9530844-0-X

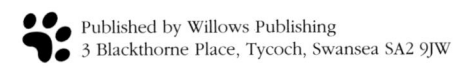

Published by Willows Publishing
3 Blackthorne Place, Tycoch, Swansea SA2 9JW

Text © Chris Keenan and Liz Barry

Photographs © Liz Barry

All food prepared for photography by Chris Keenan and Darren Thomas.

Food Photography credited to Siân Turner and David Nicol,
Students on BTEC National Diploma in Design course at Swansea College
Course Manager - Roger Tiley

Black and white photographs © refer to acknowledgments.

Title page 'The Cockle Pickers' © Andrew Forbes

All rights reserved. No part of this work may be reproduced or transmitted in any form or by any means, electronic, mechanical including photocopying, recording or otherwise stored on a retrieval system of any nature without the written permission of the copyright holders in advance.

Designed and typeset by DWJ Colourprint Design Studio
Printed by DWJ Colourprint

Back cover picture: *Swansea's old, Swansea's new, watched over by the moon.*